The Fox Book

A FOXY COLORING BOOK FOR EVERYONE

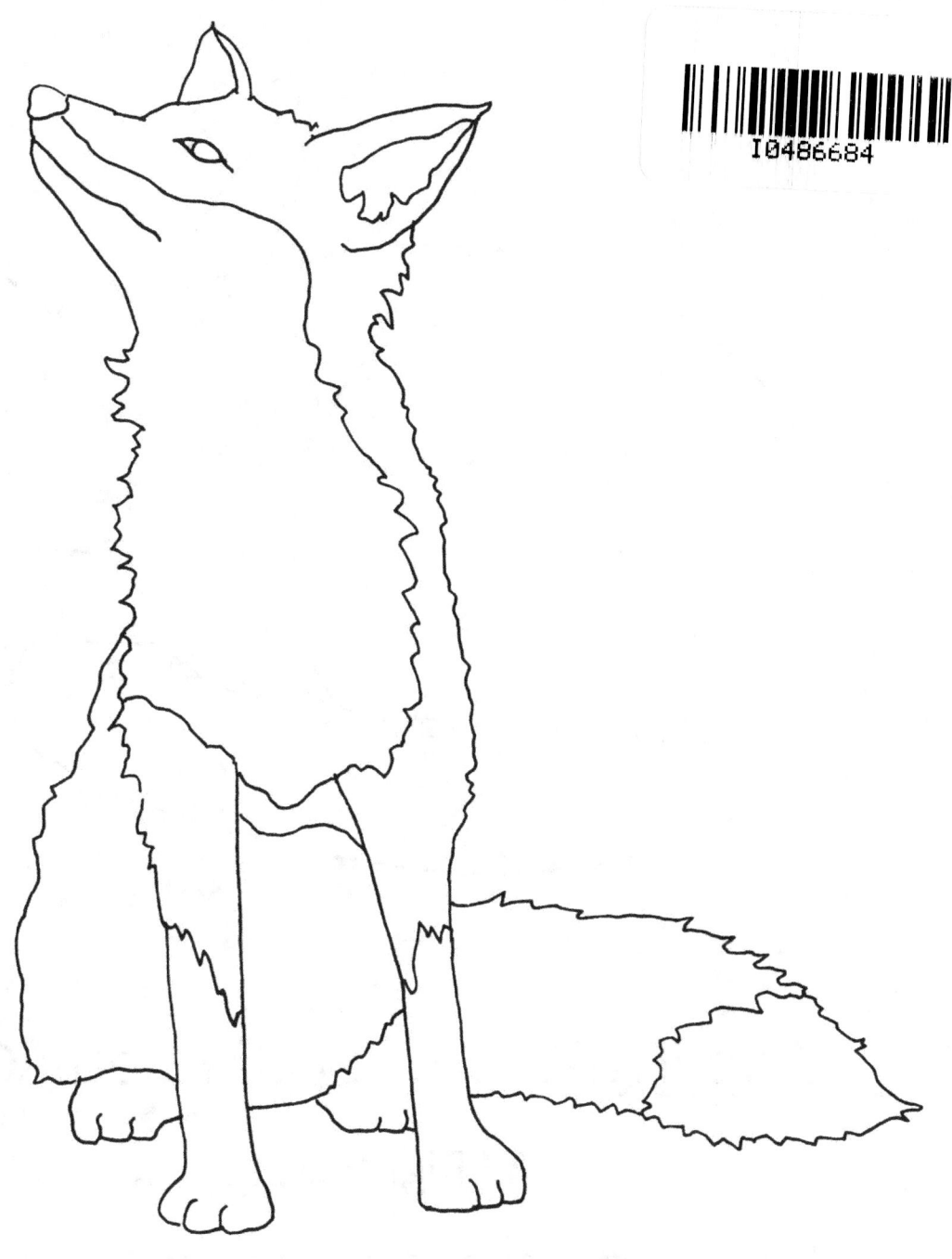

Drawings by Kimberly Garvey

Kimberlygarvey.com

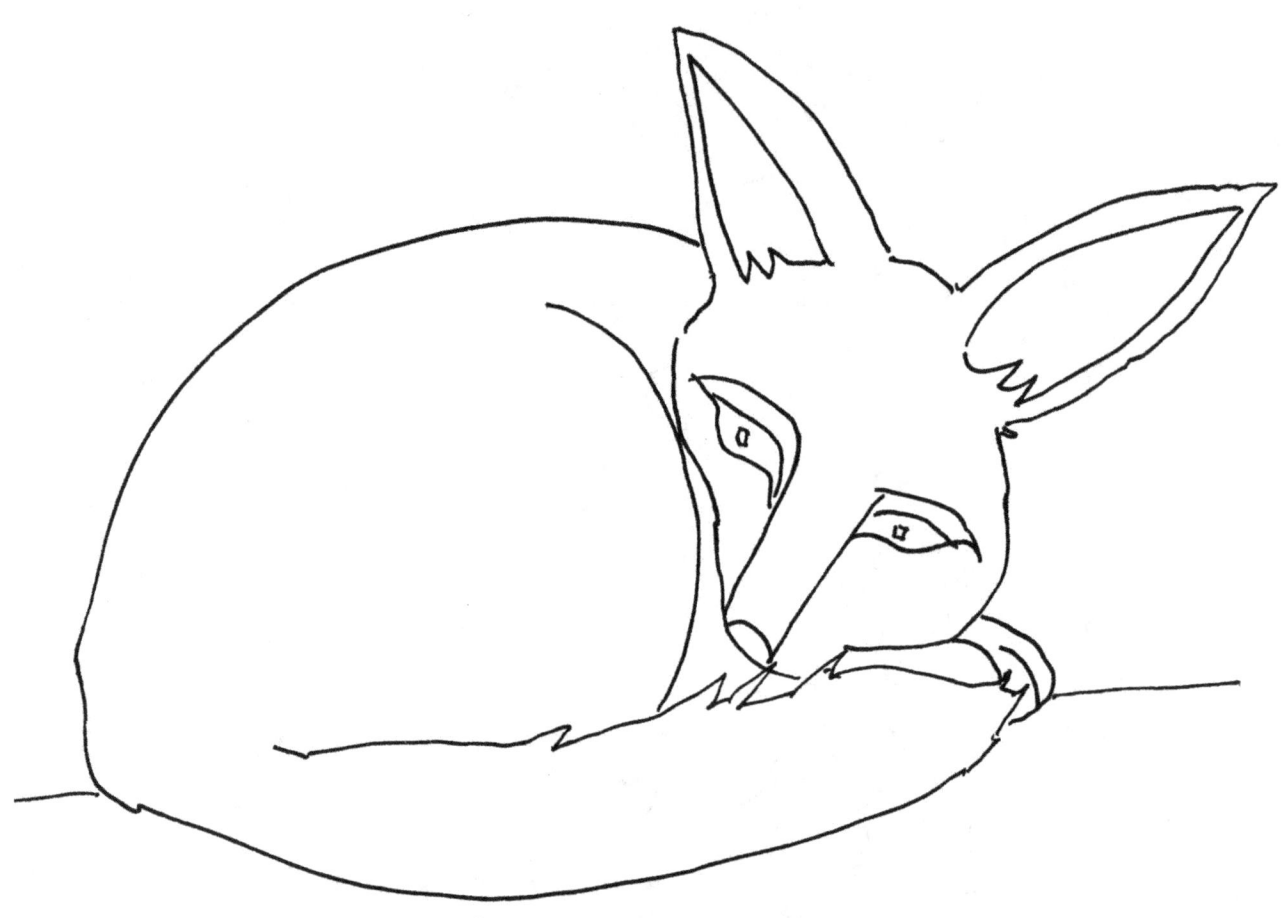

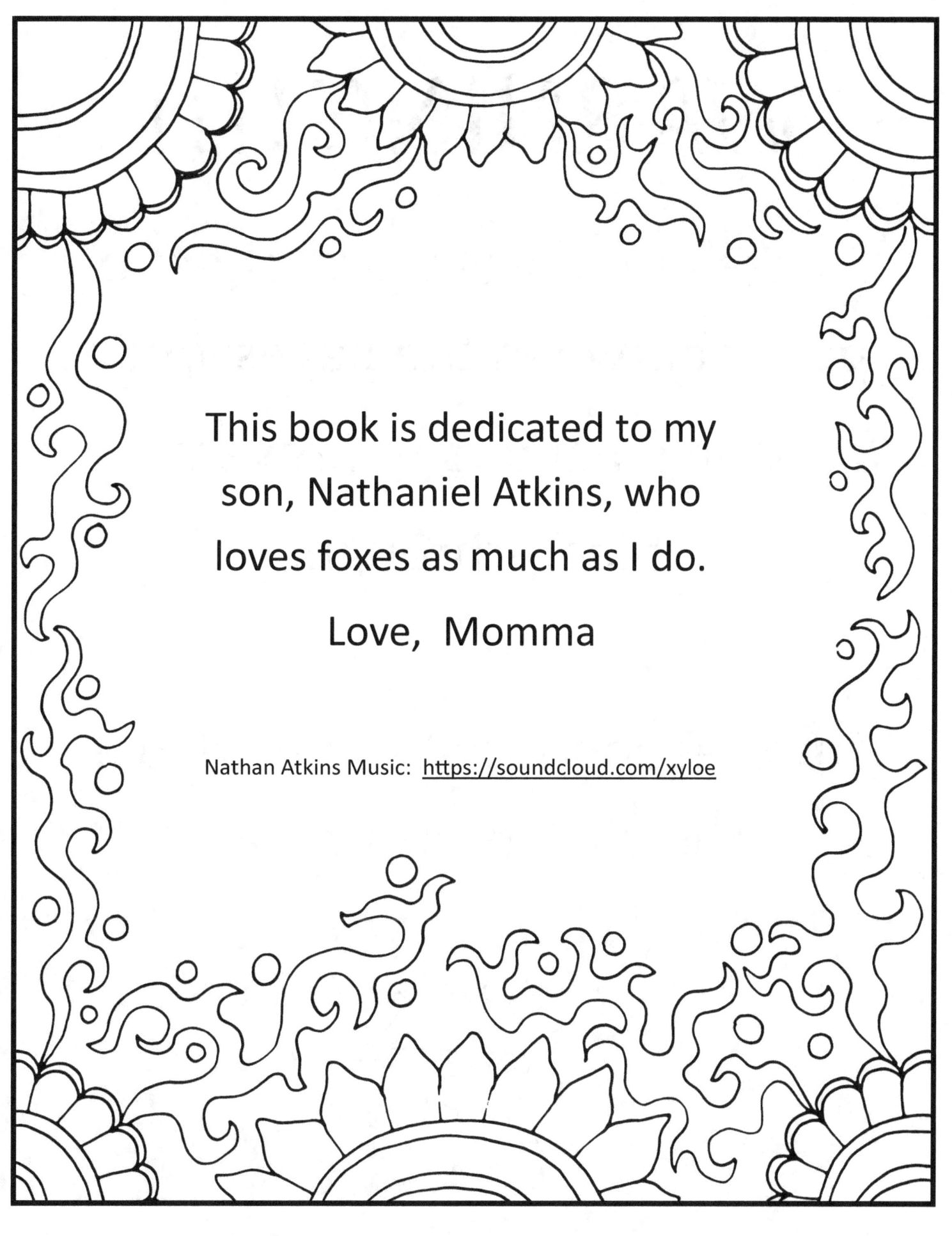

This book is dedicated to my son, Nathaniel Atkins, who loves foxes as much as I do.

Love, Momma

Nathan Atkins Music: https://soundcloud.com/xyloe

WARNING!!!!

Please put a protection sheet of paper between the pages when using markers to prevent bleed-through.

A protection sheet is included at the back of this book.

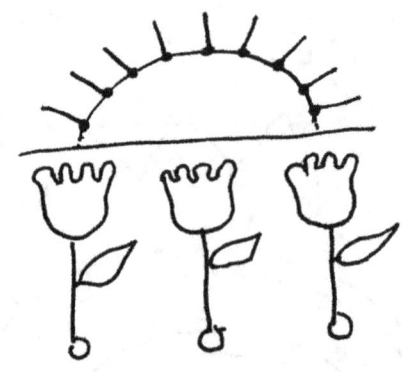

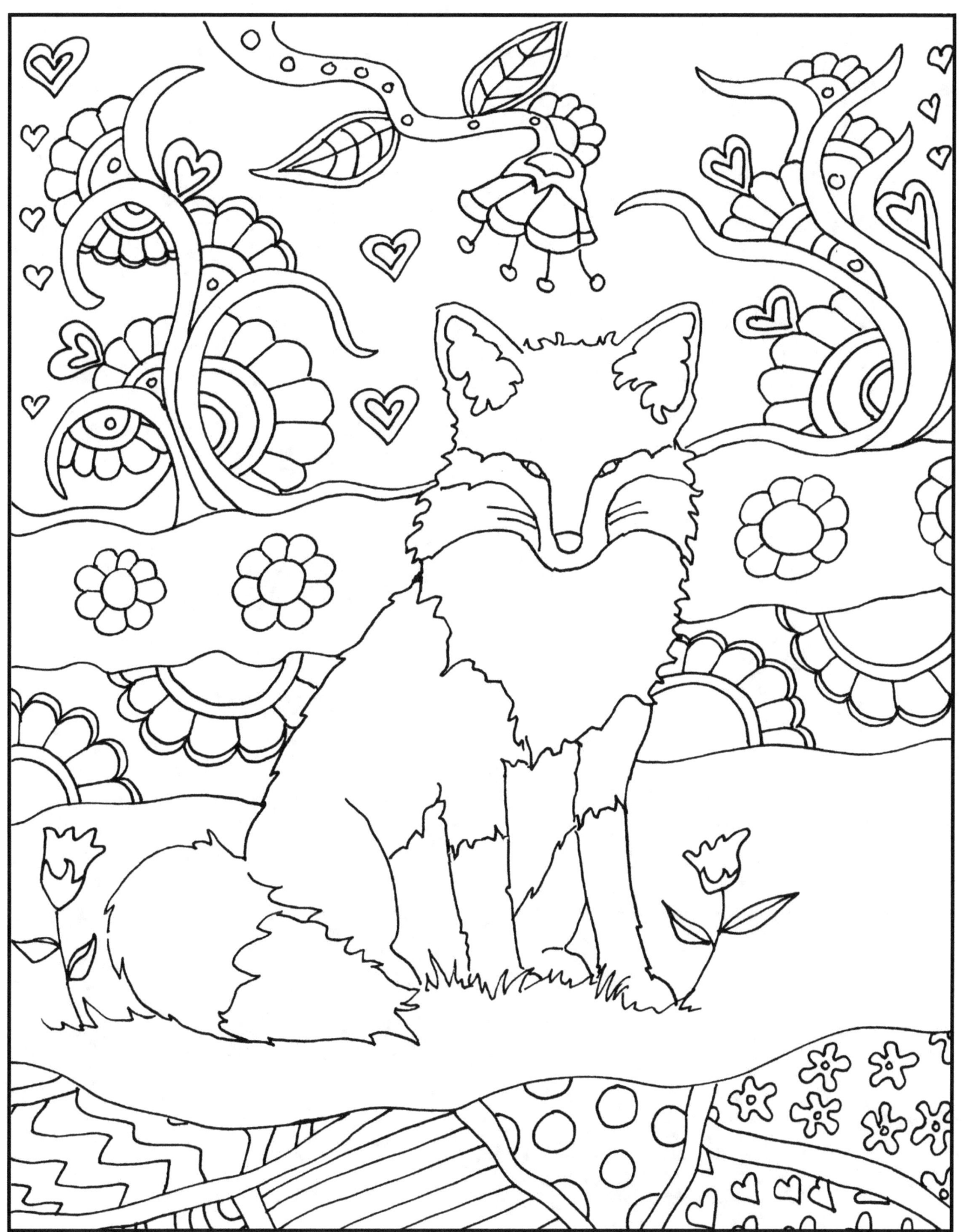

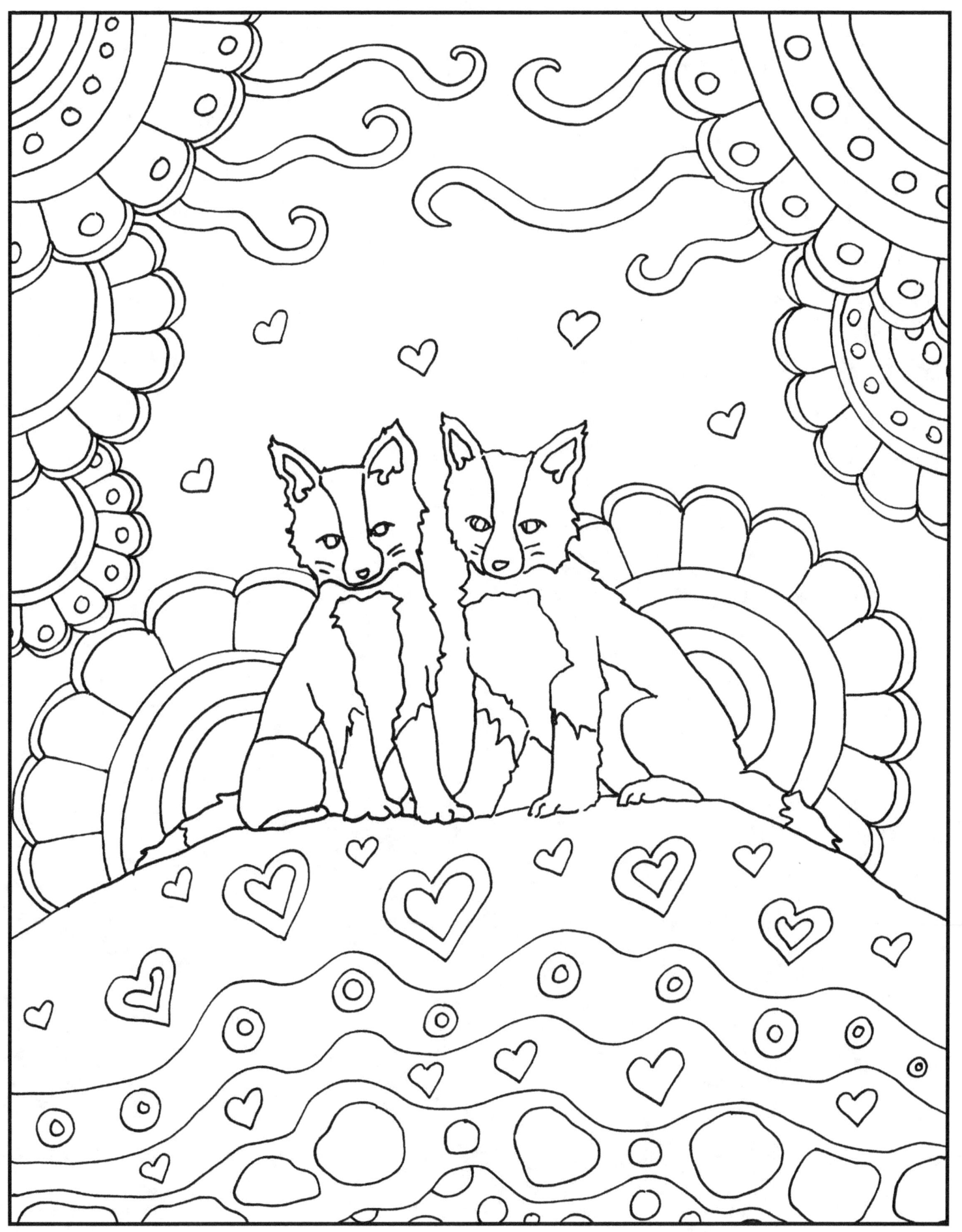

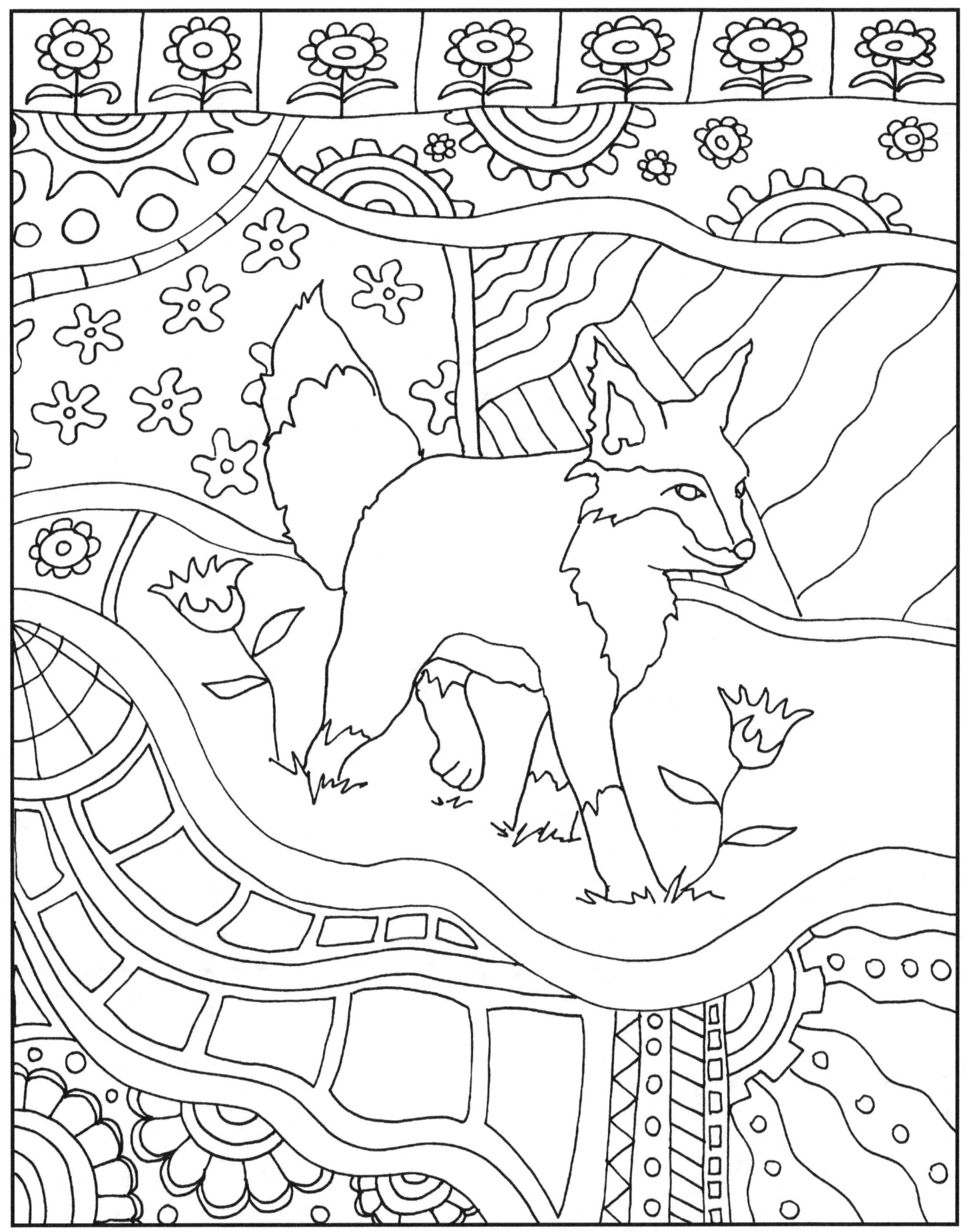

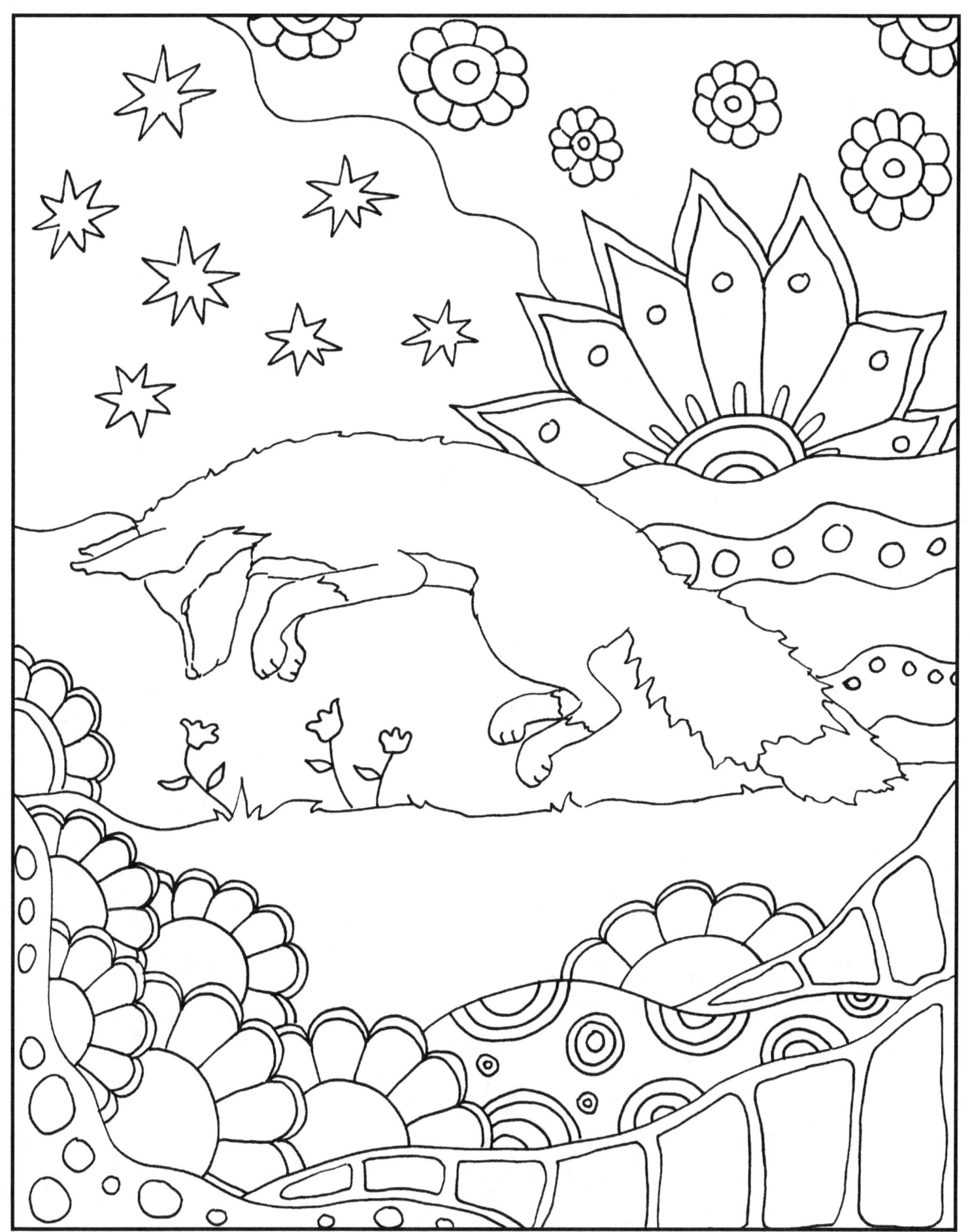

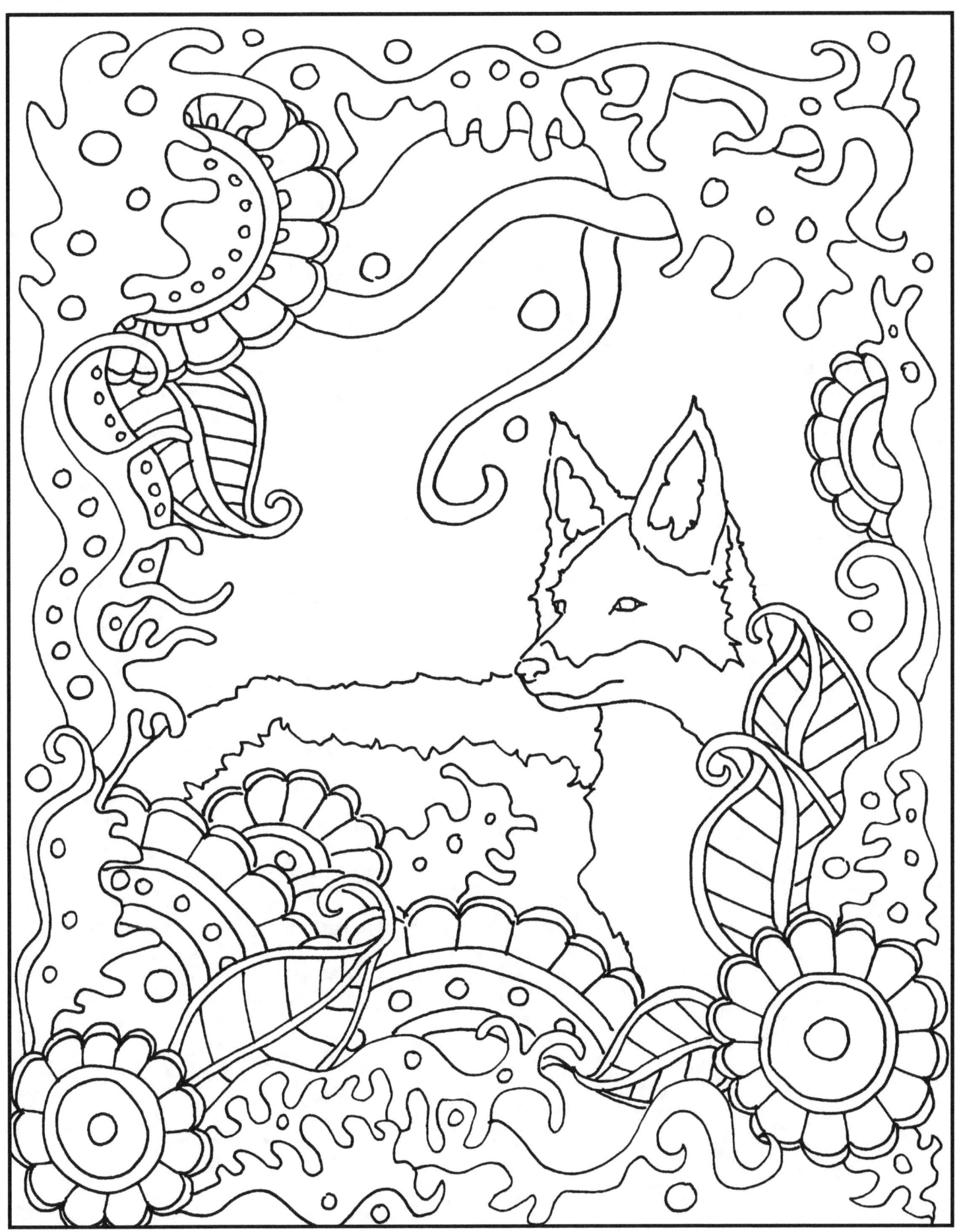

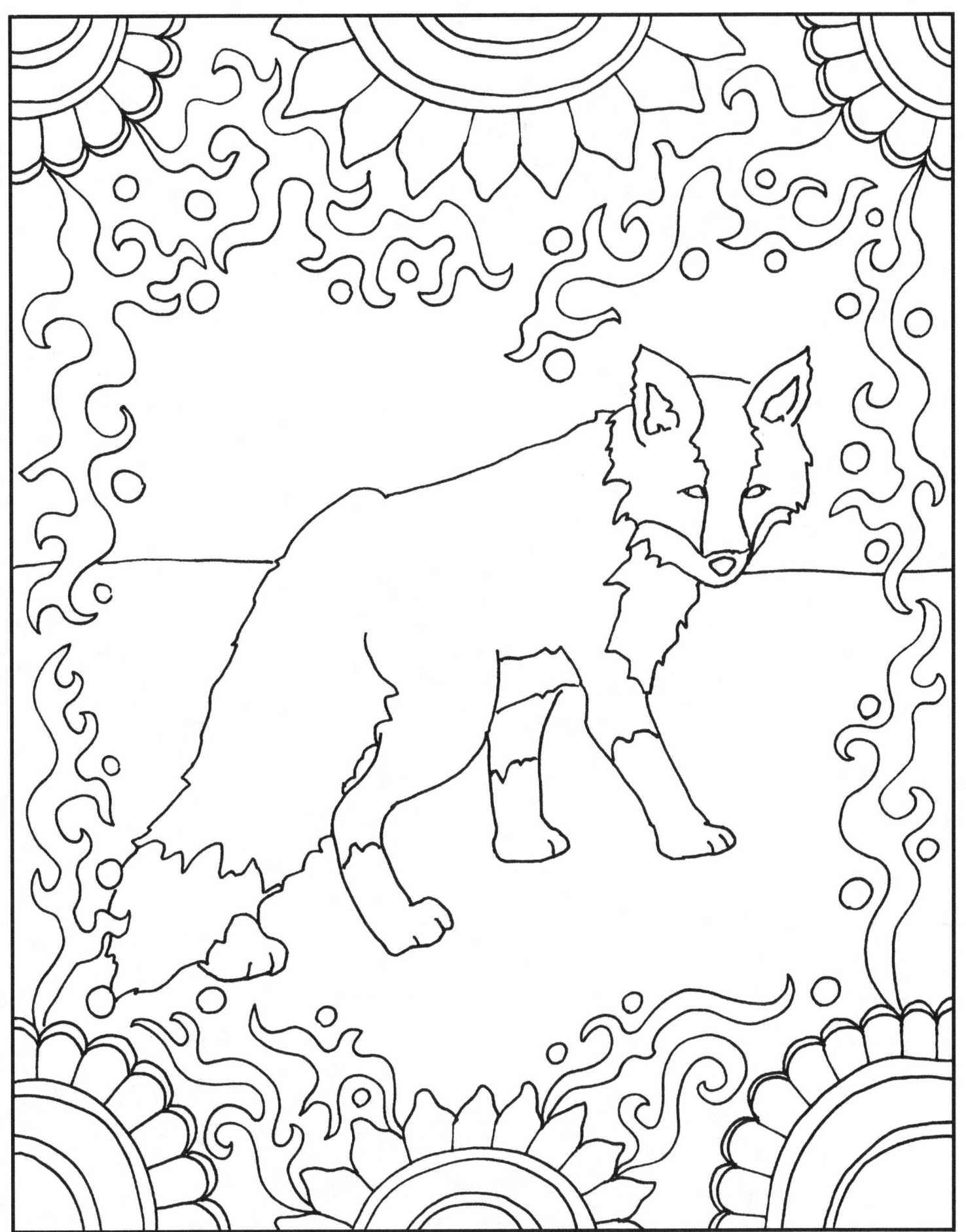

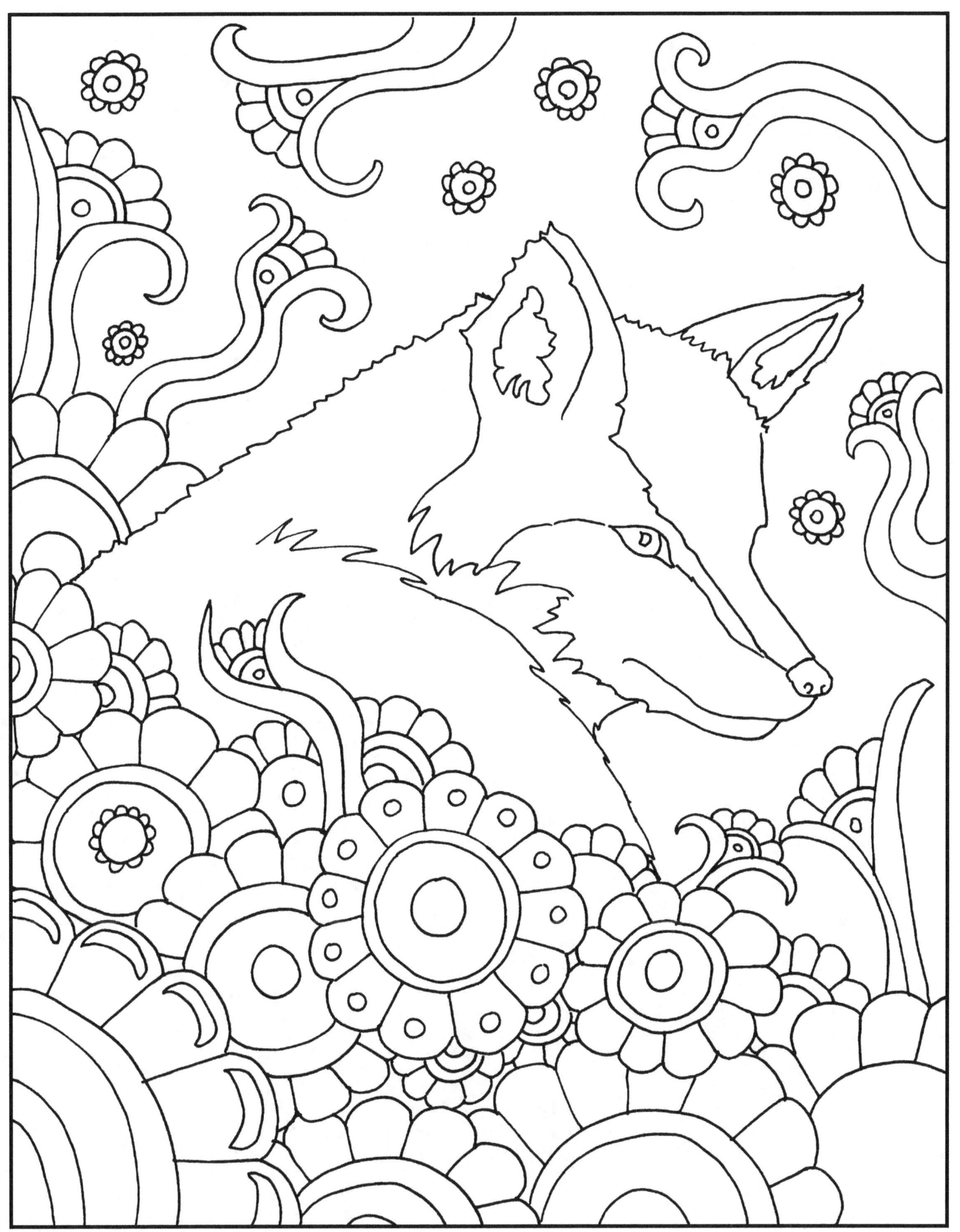

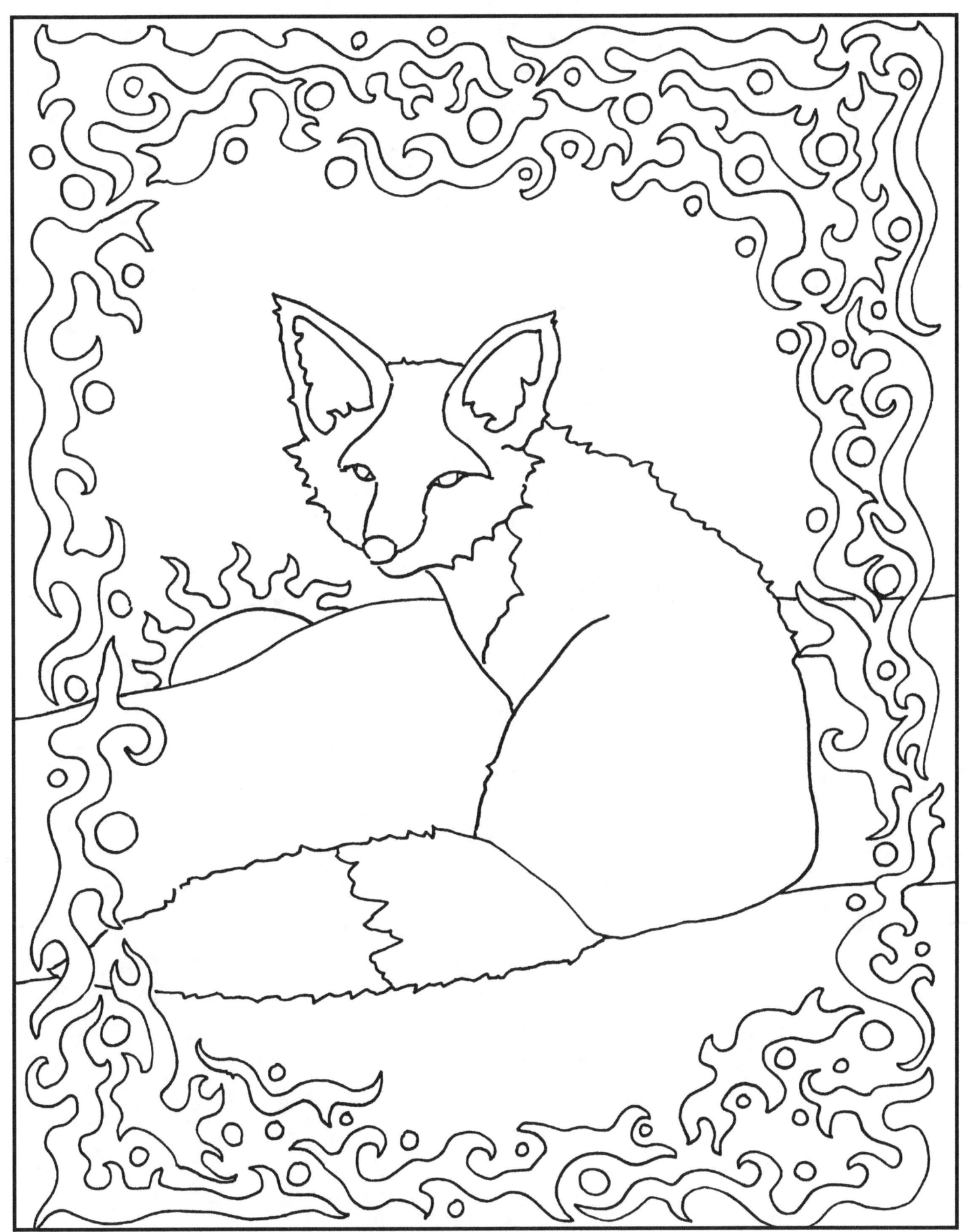

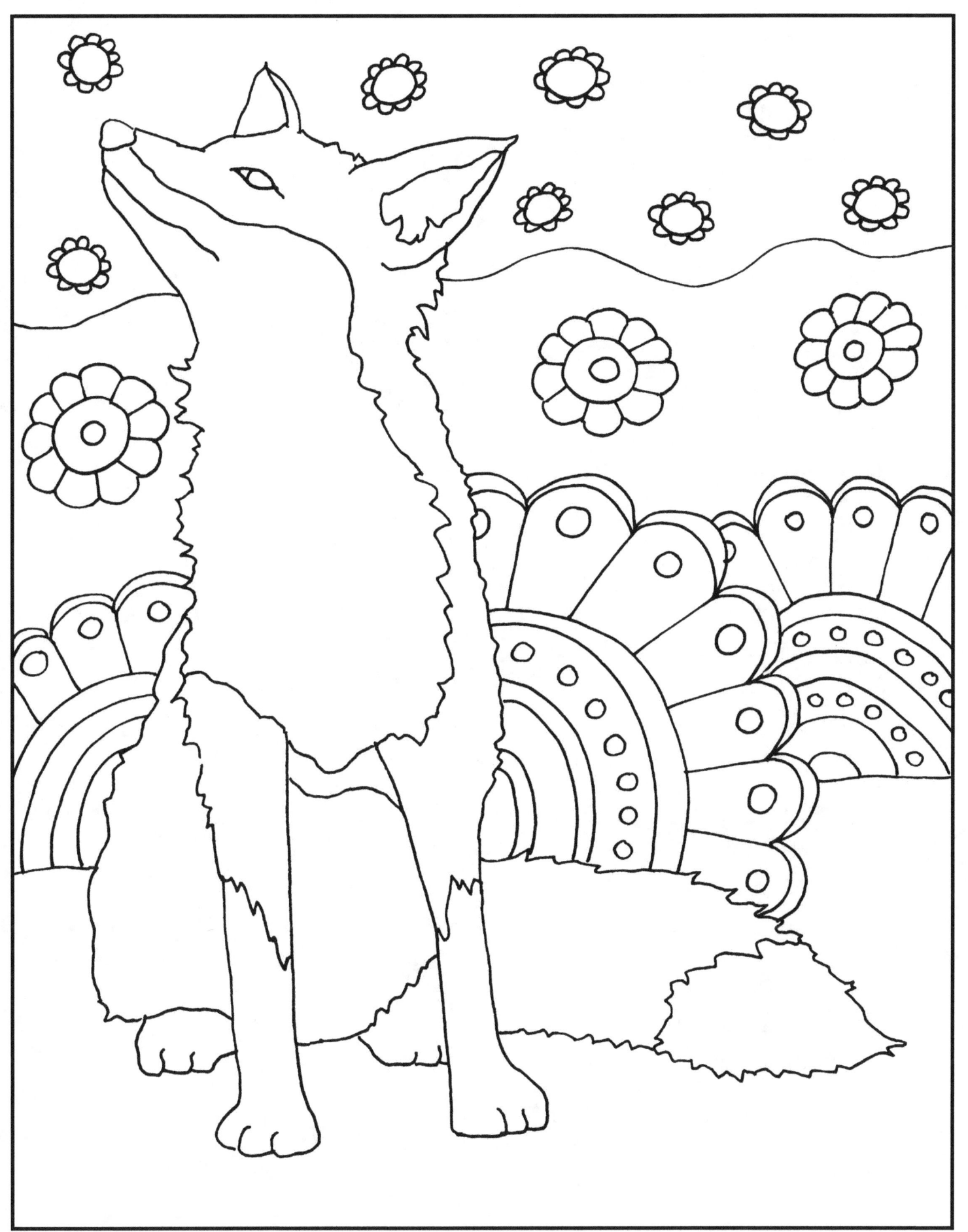

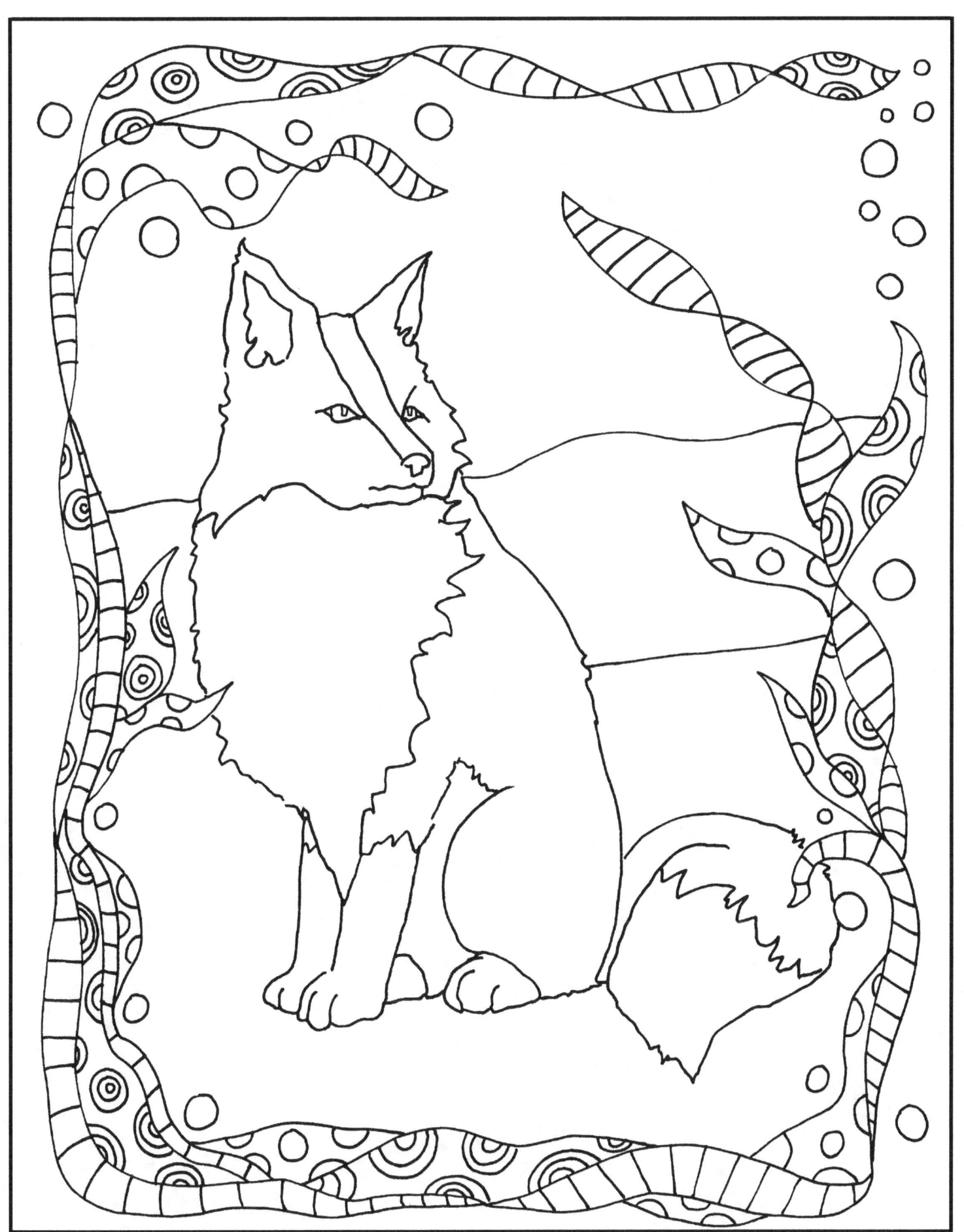

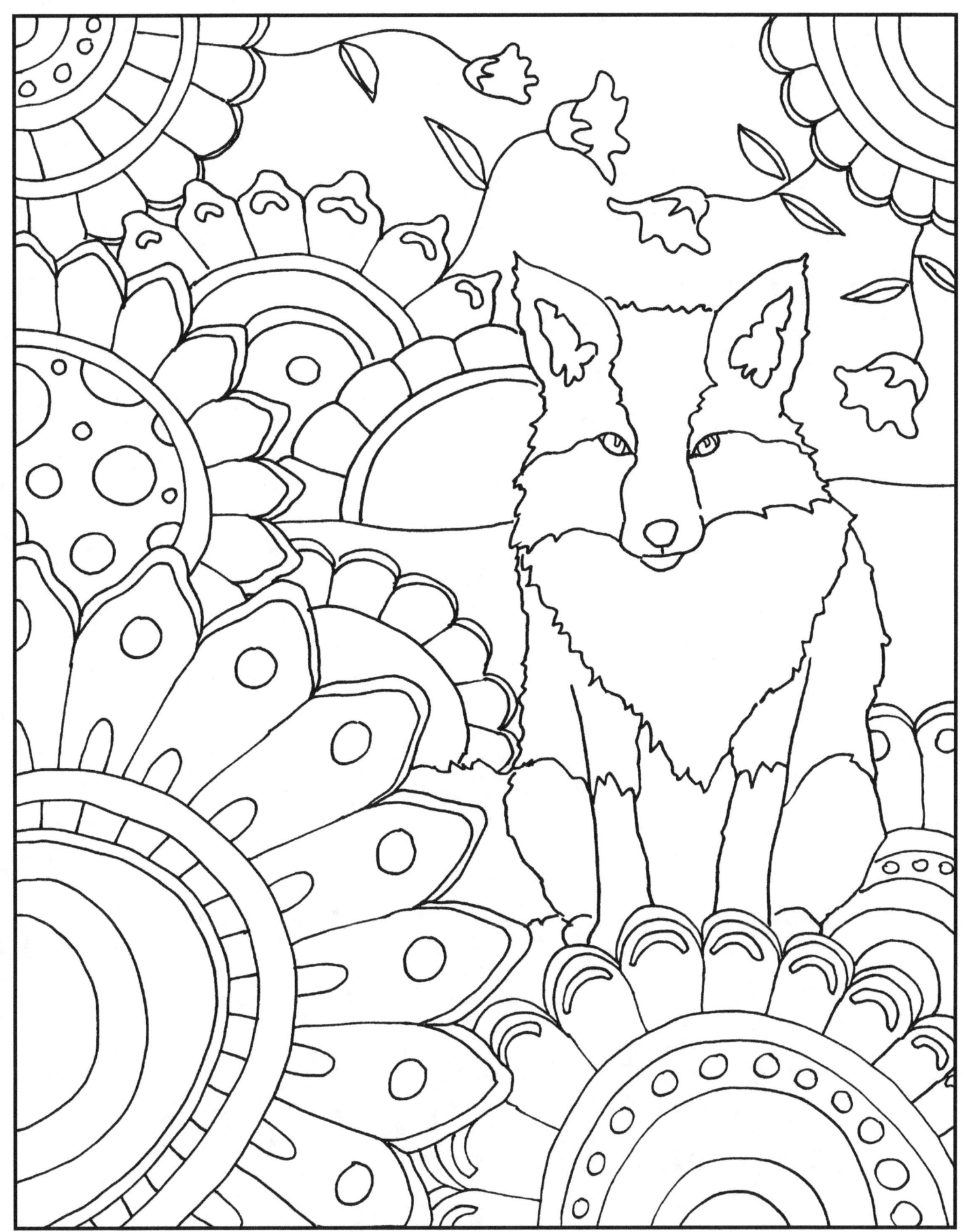

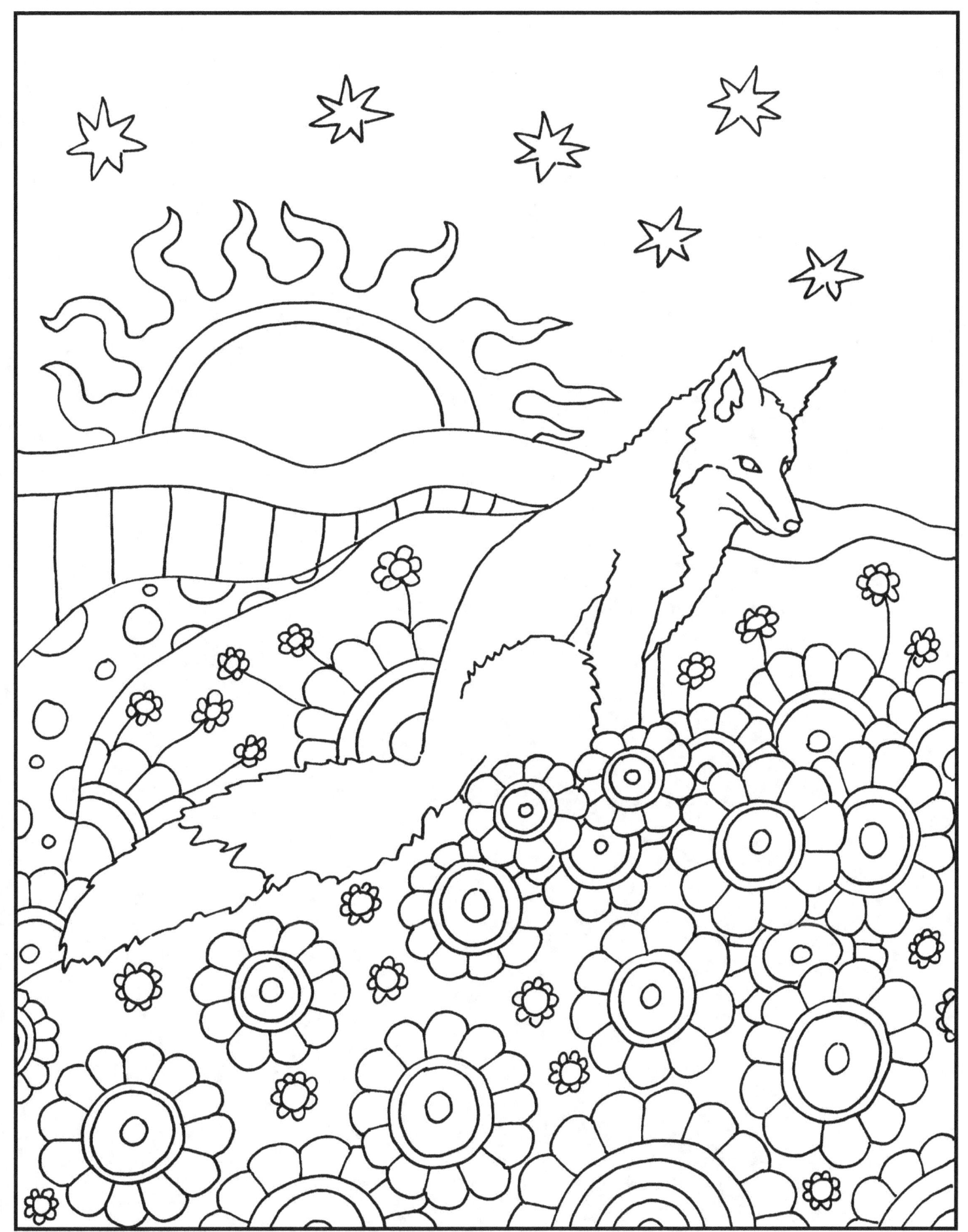

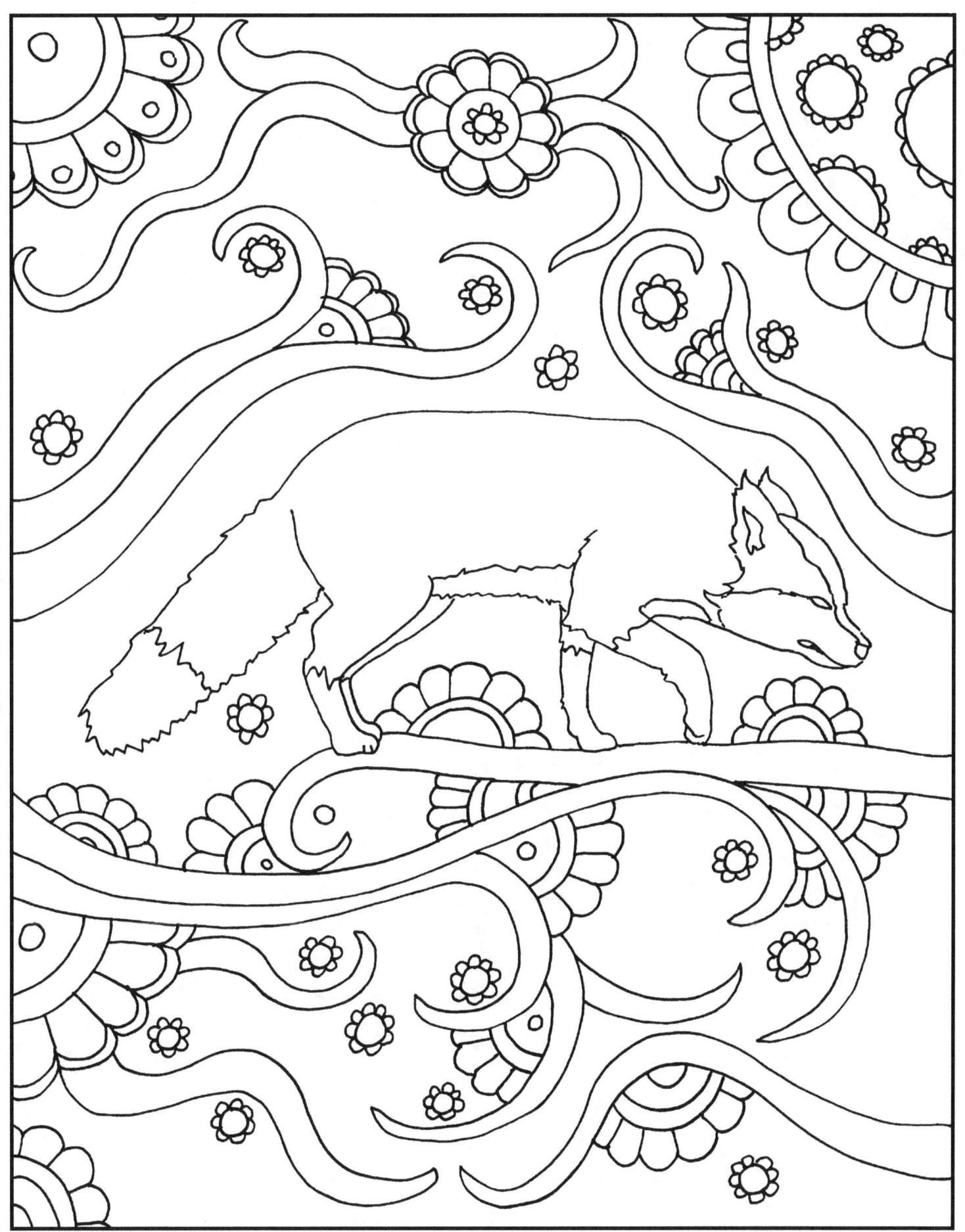

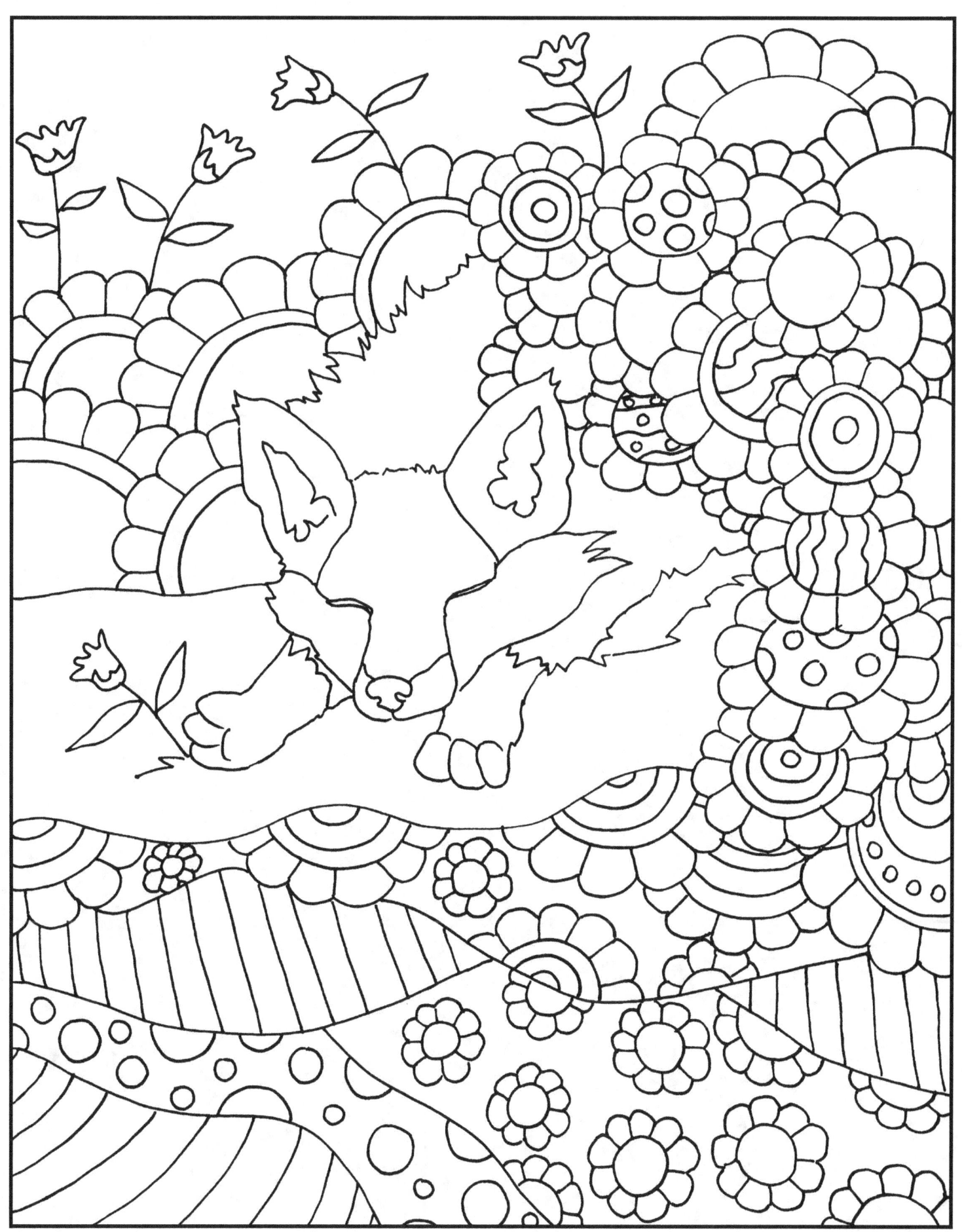

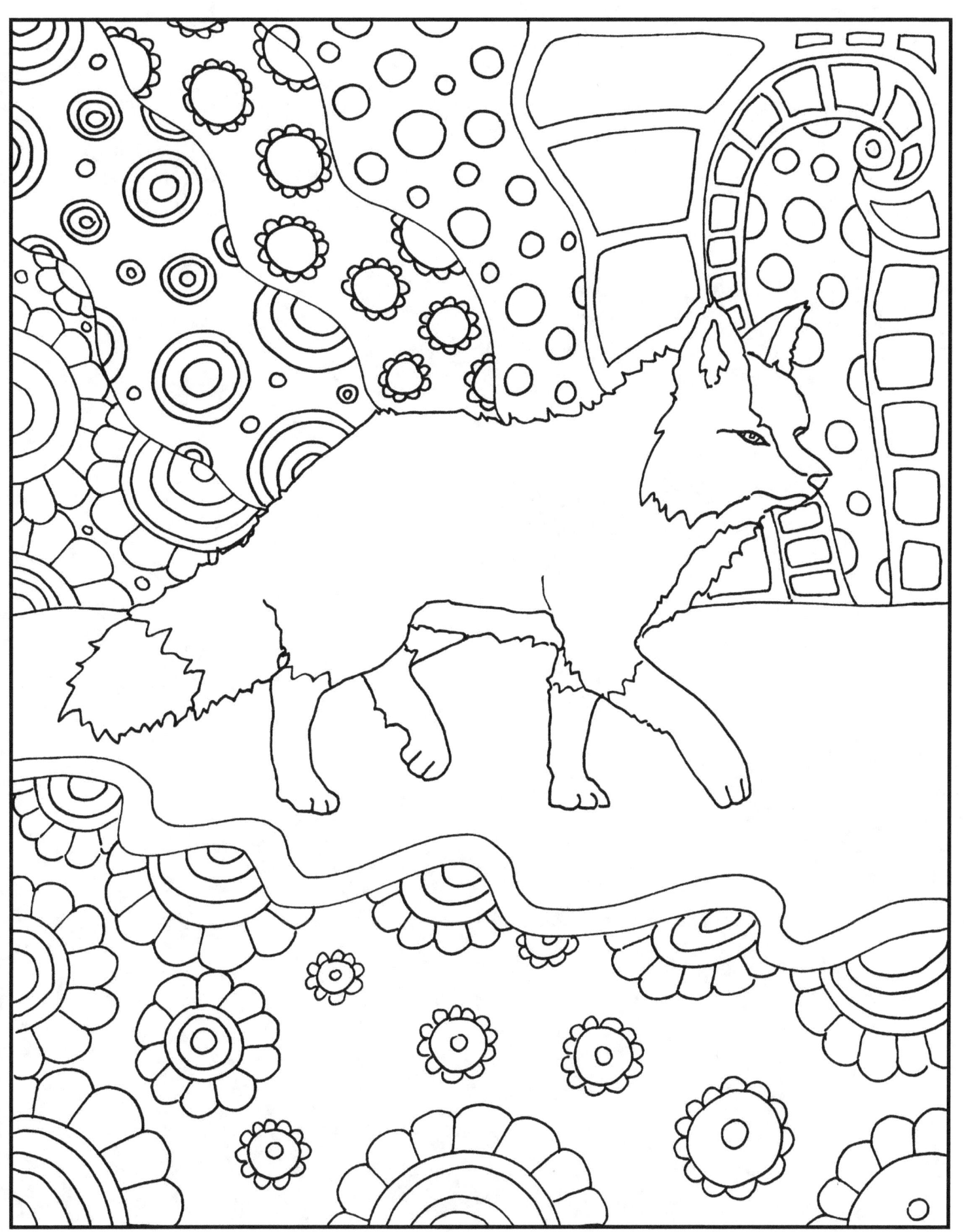

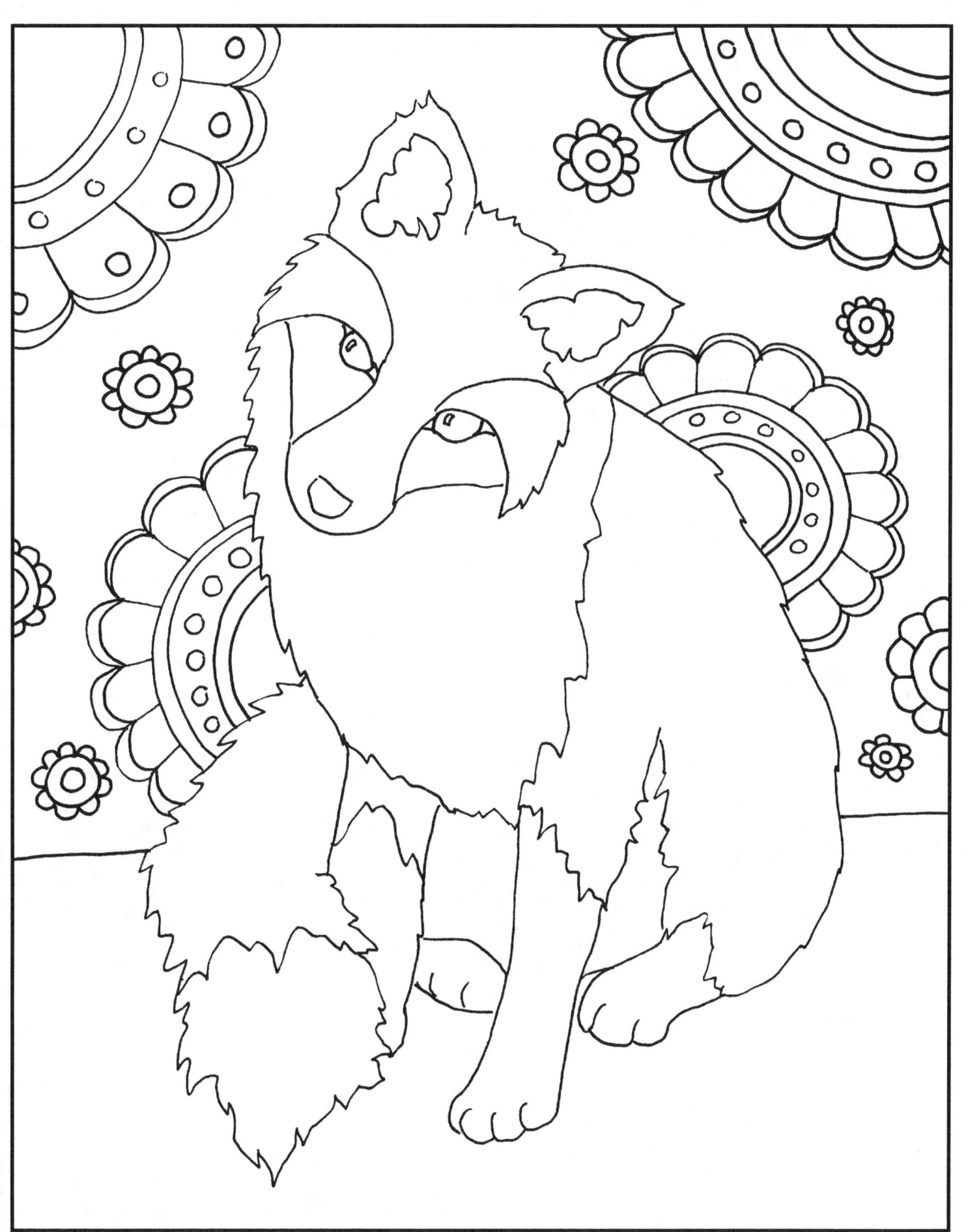

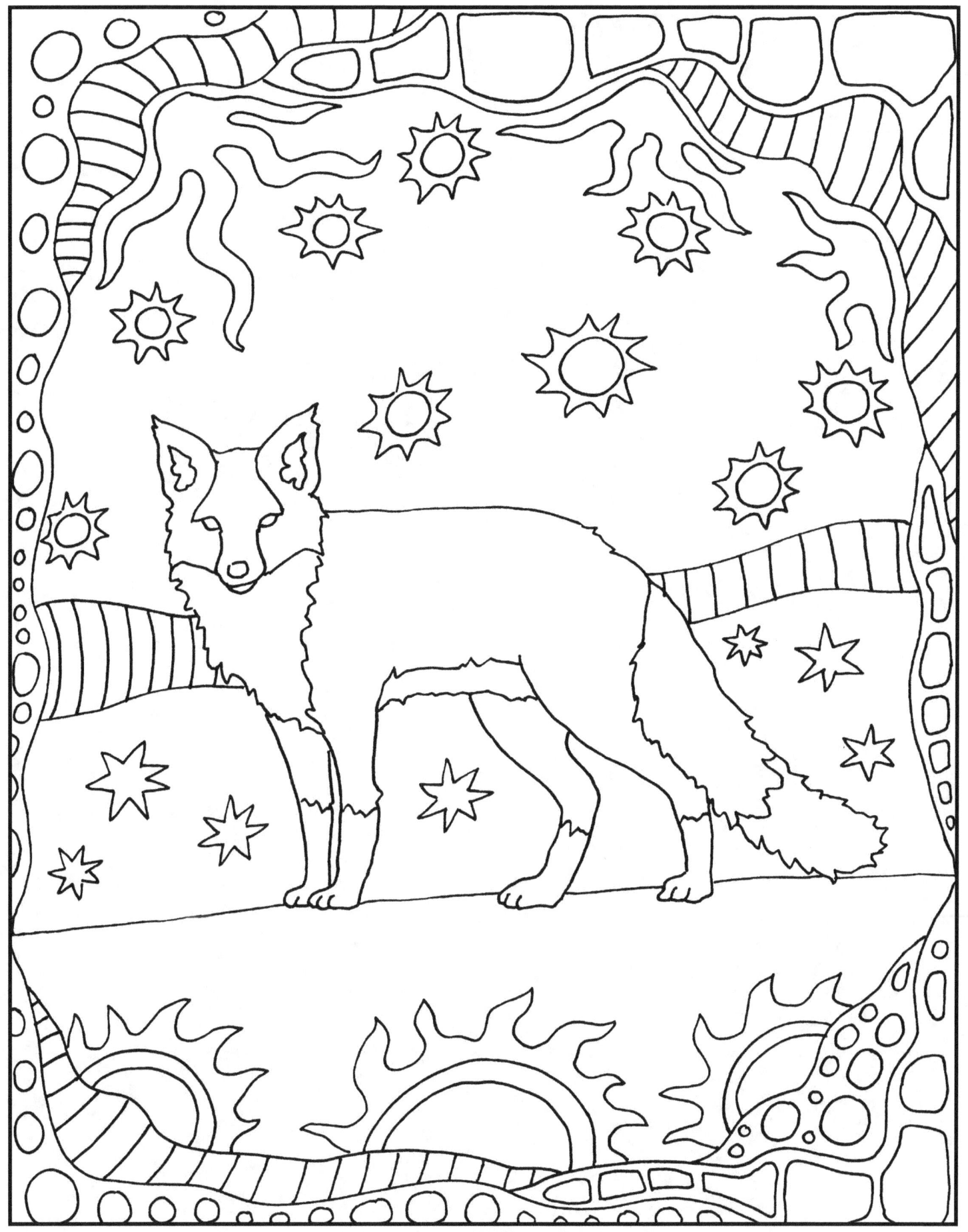

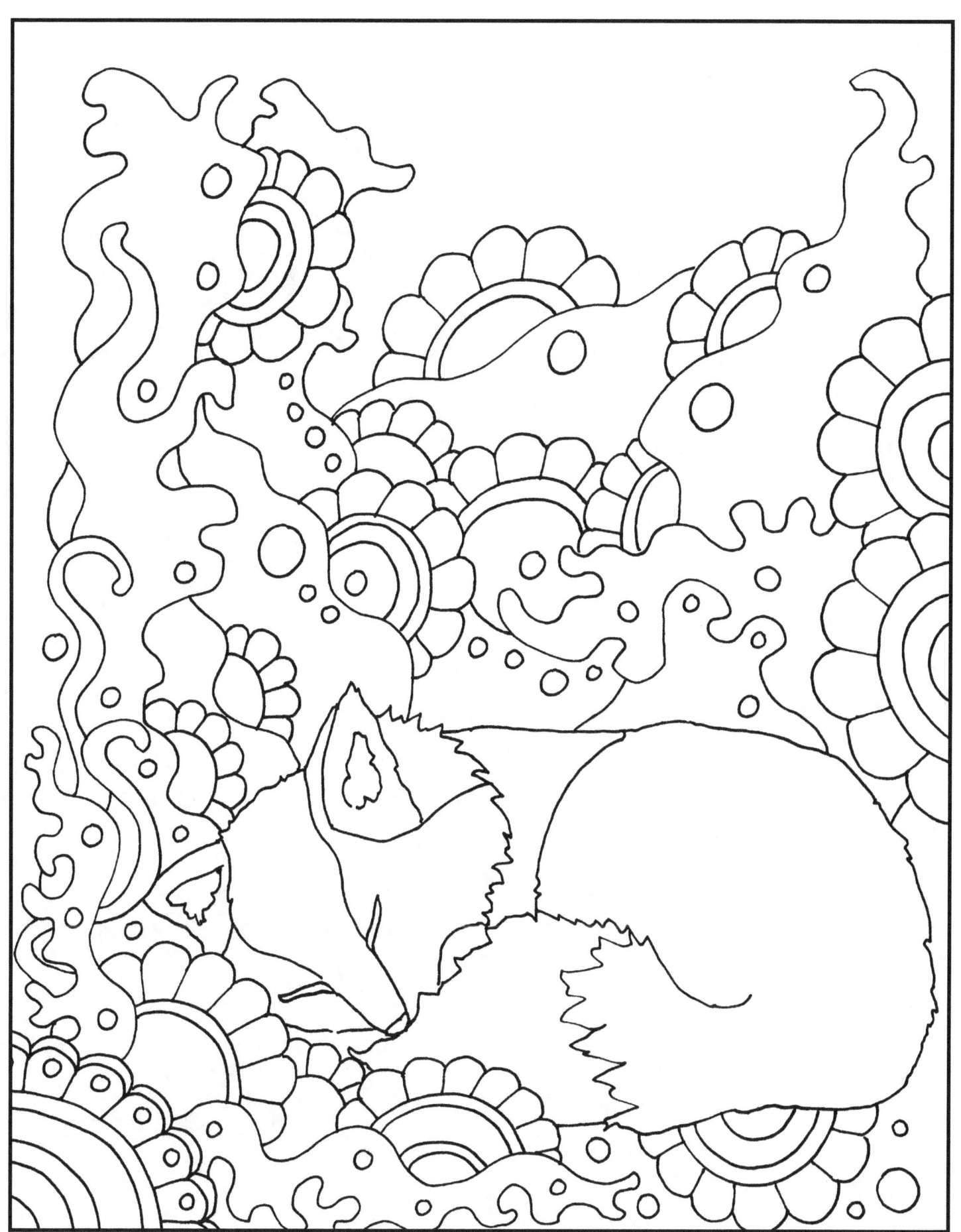

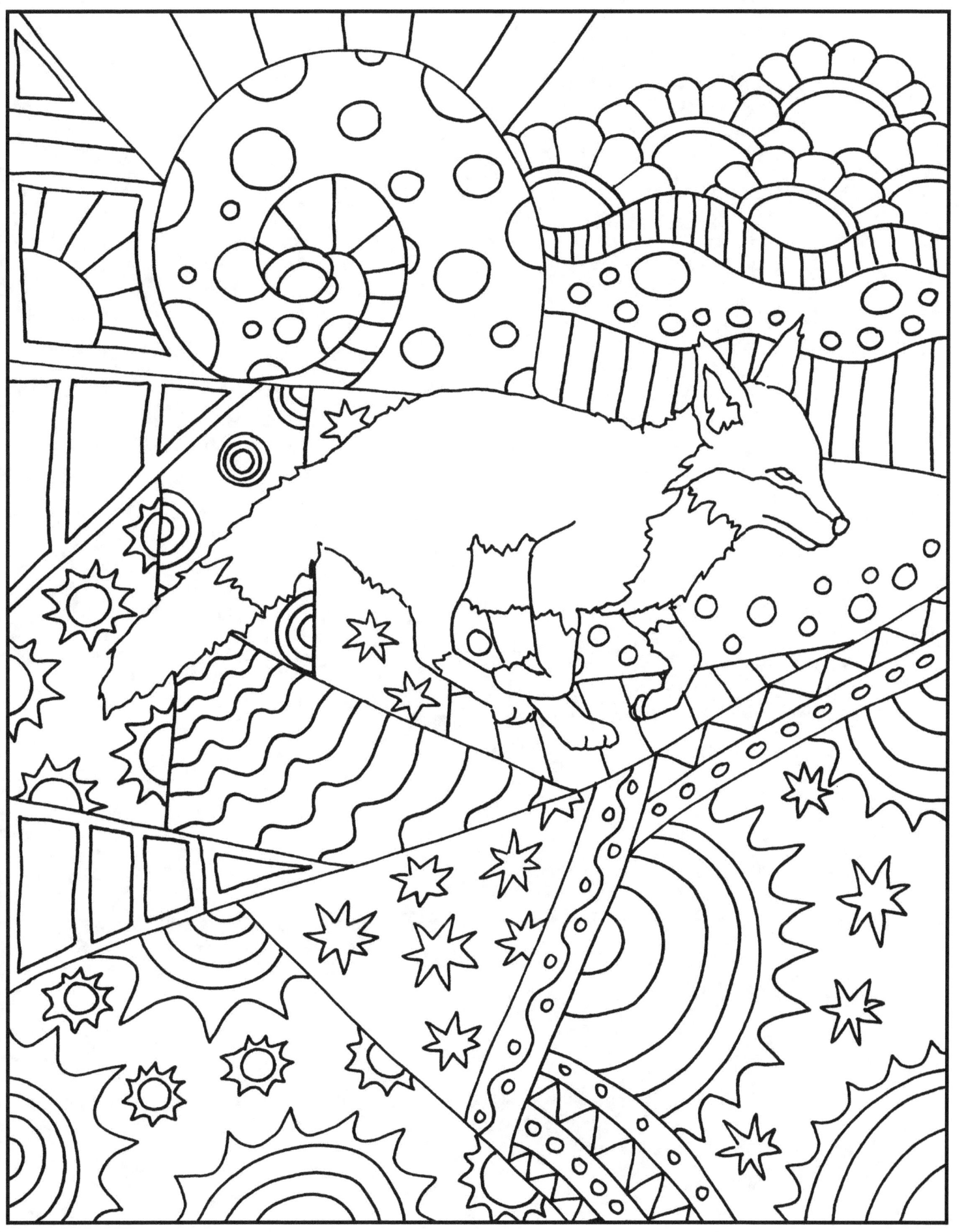

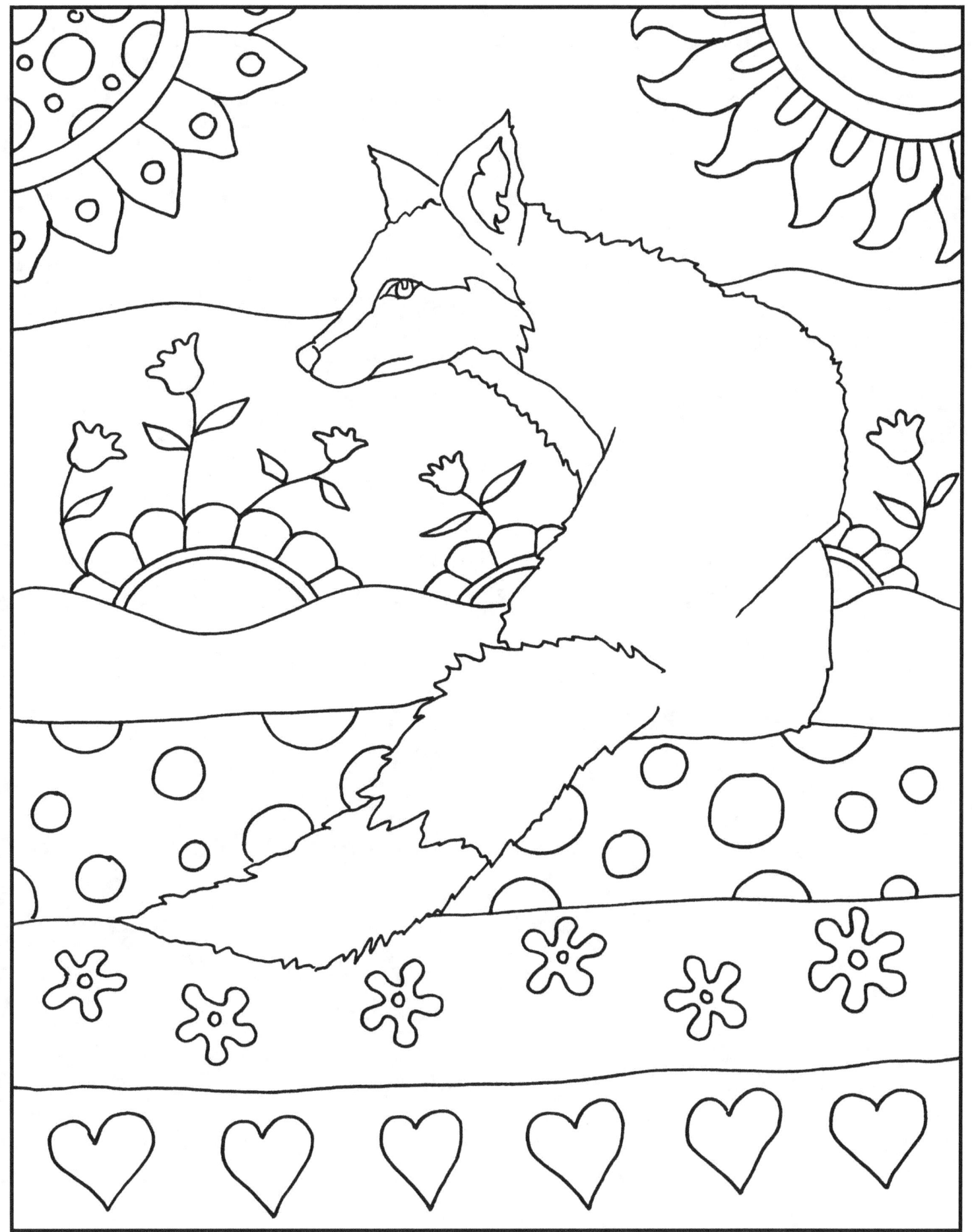

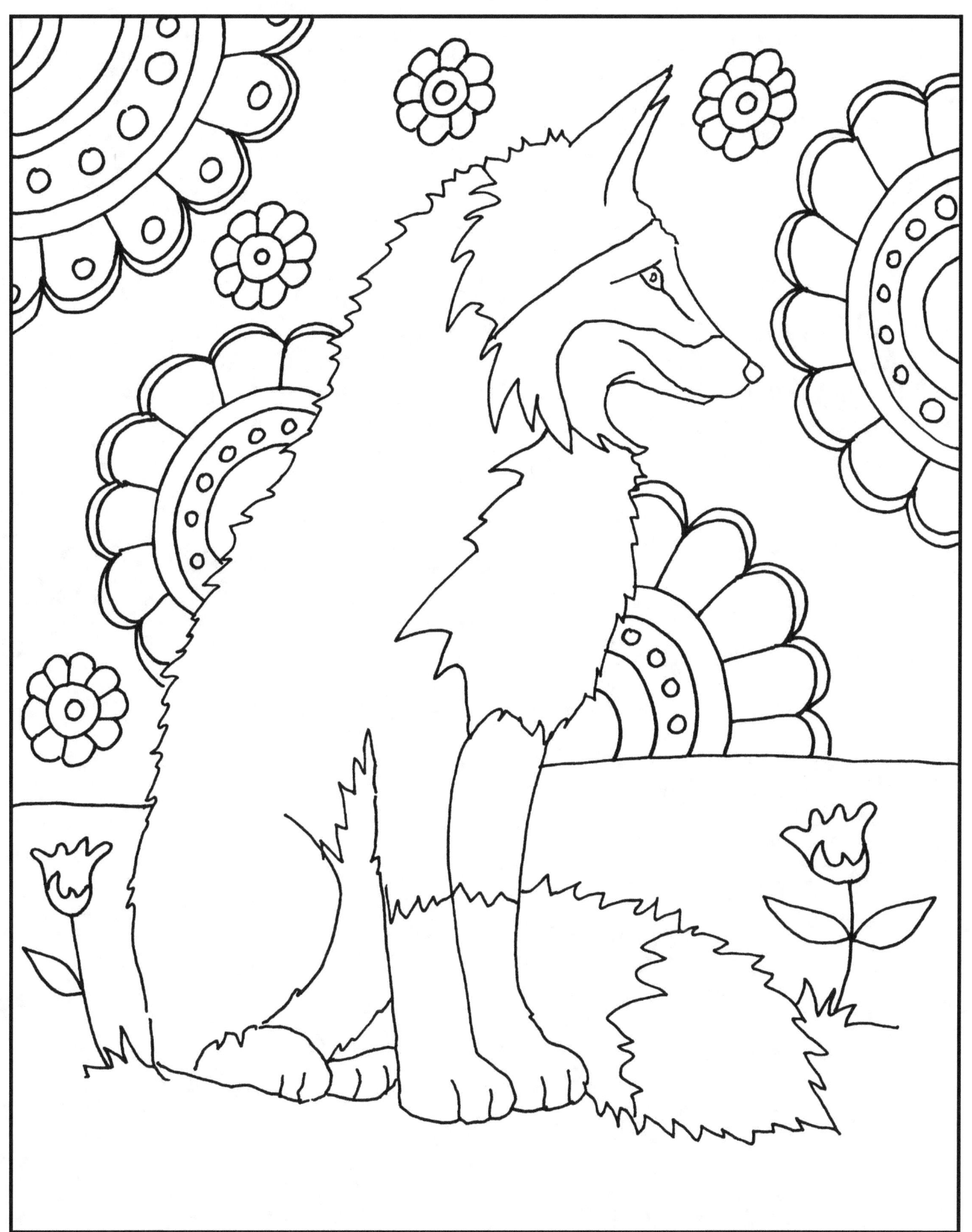

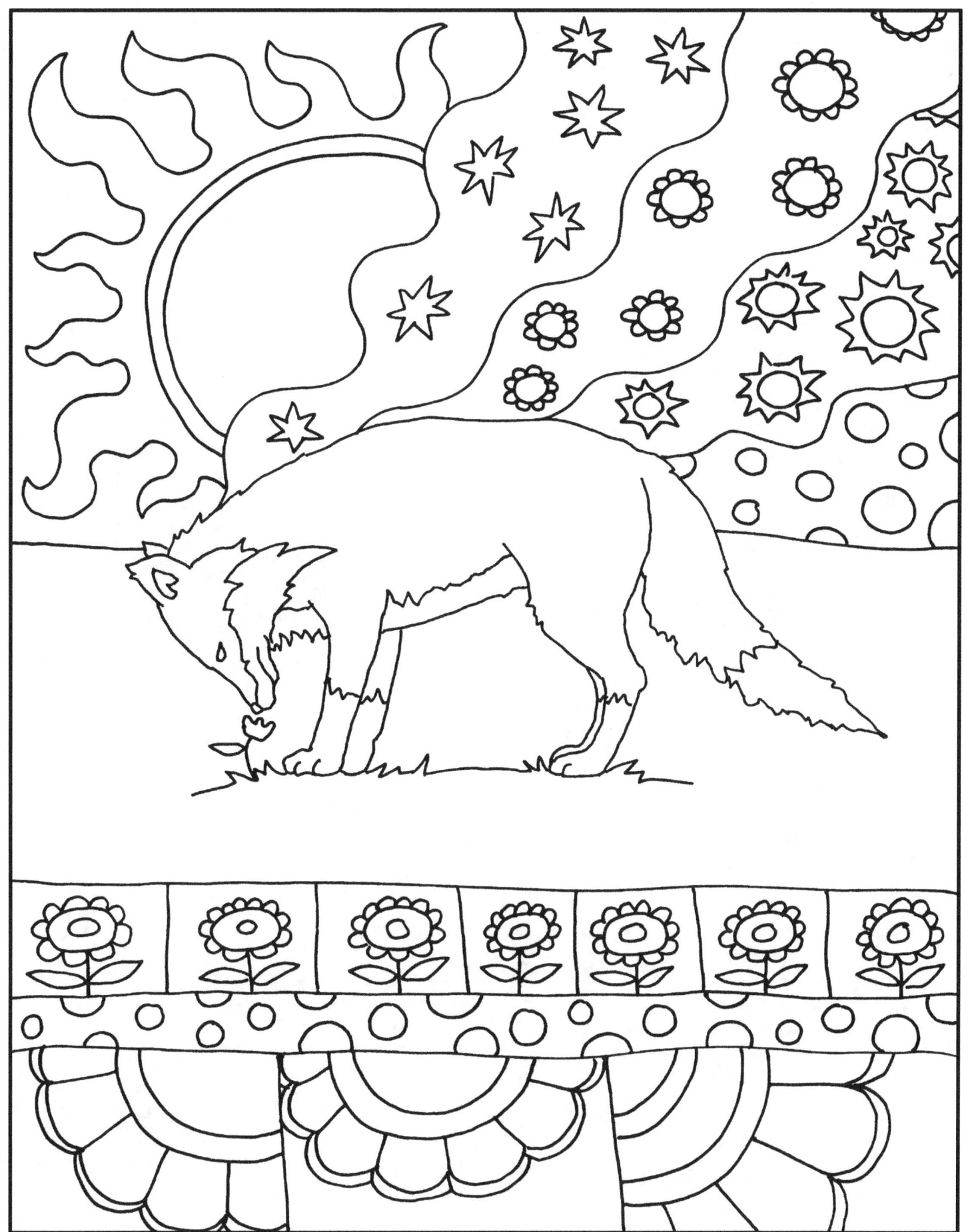

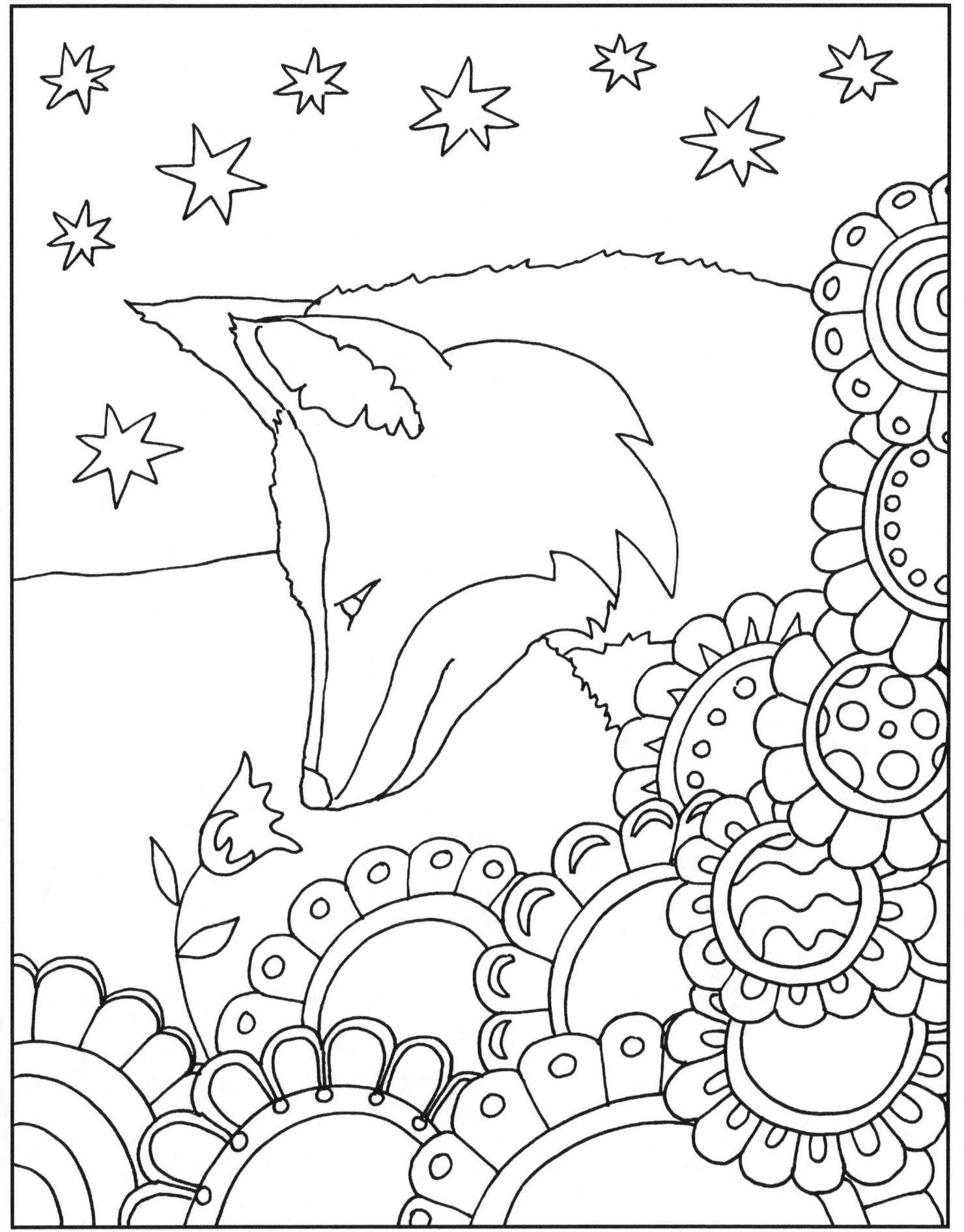

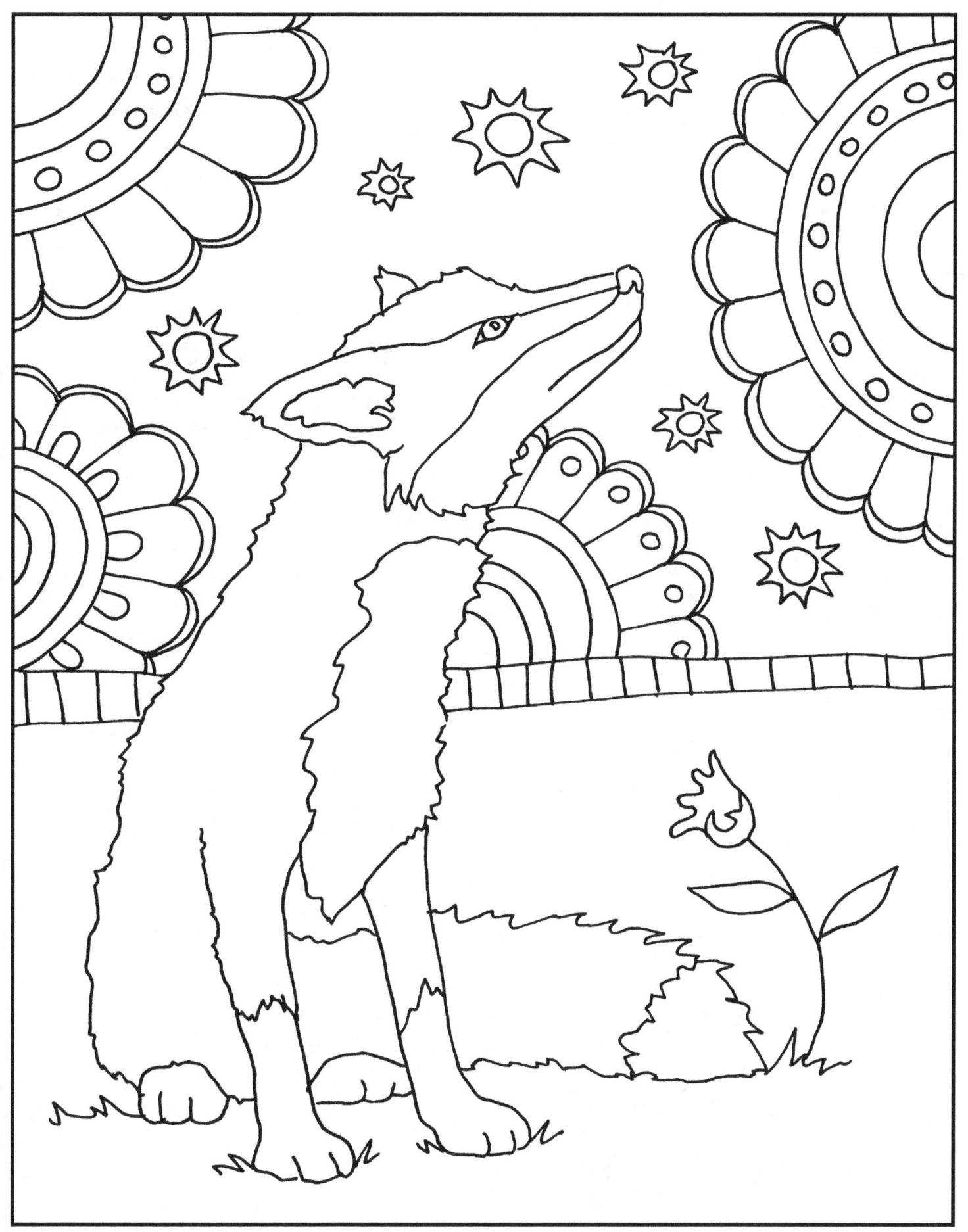

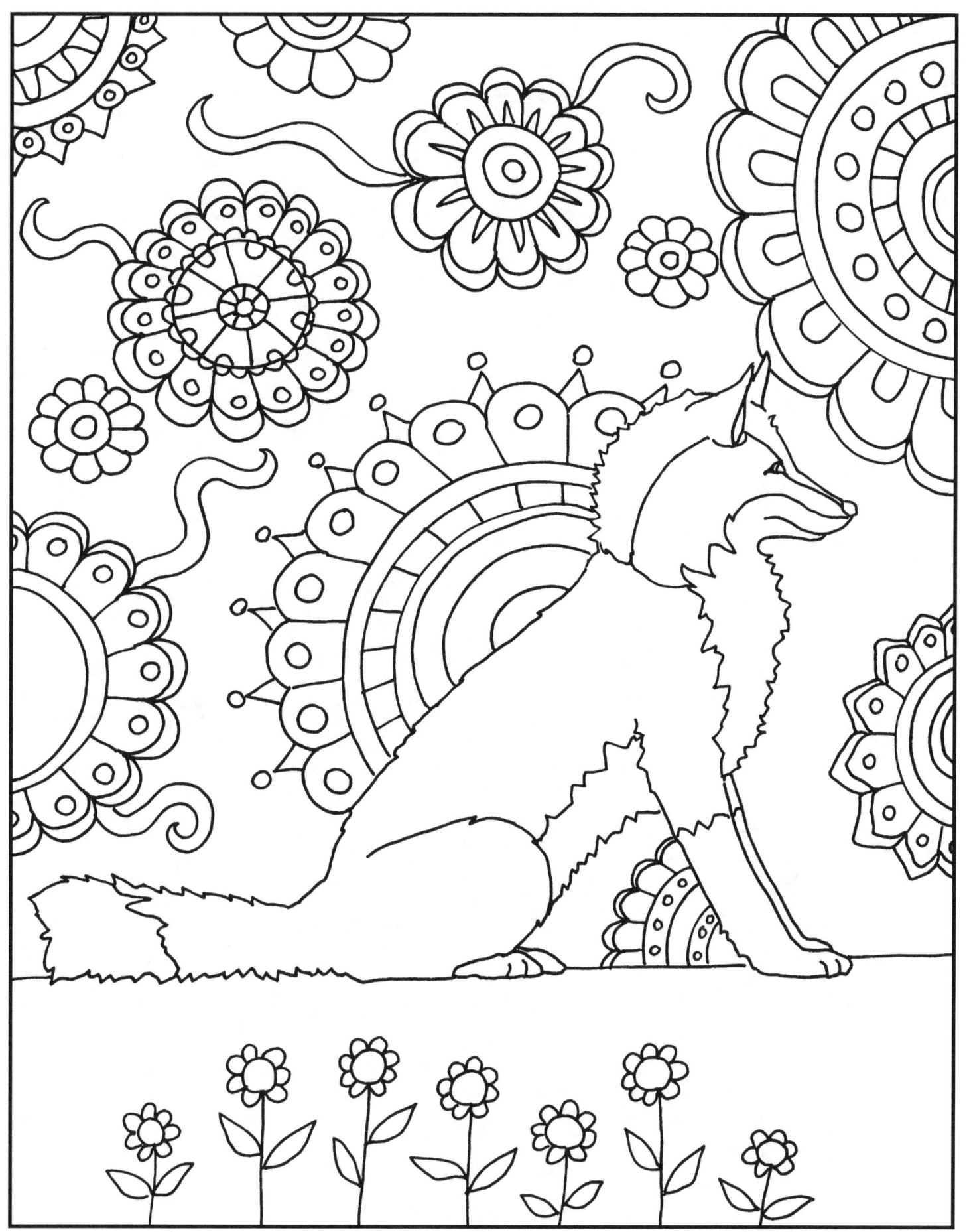

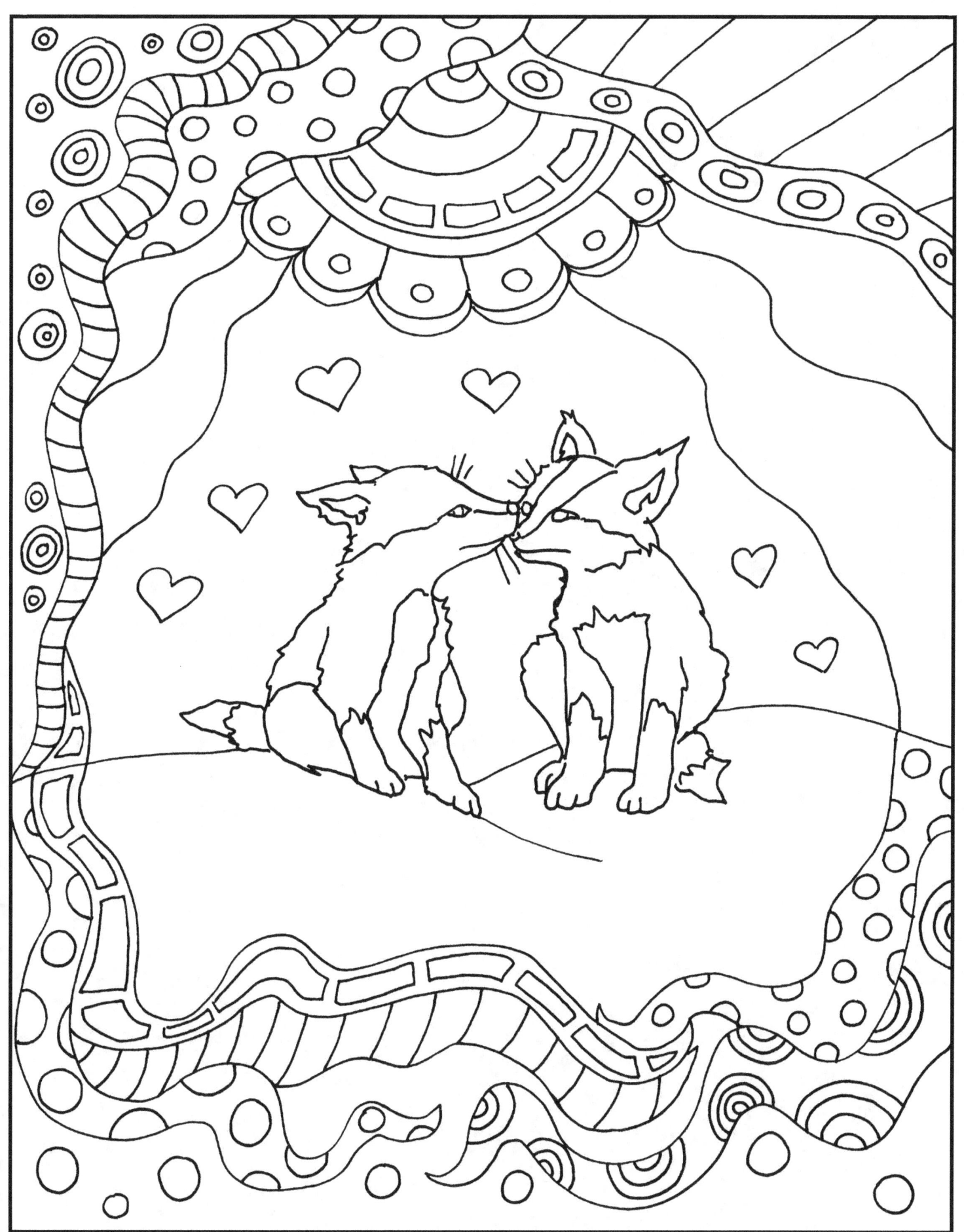

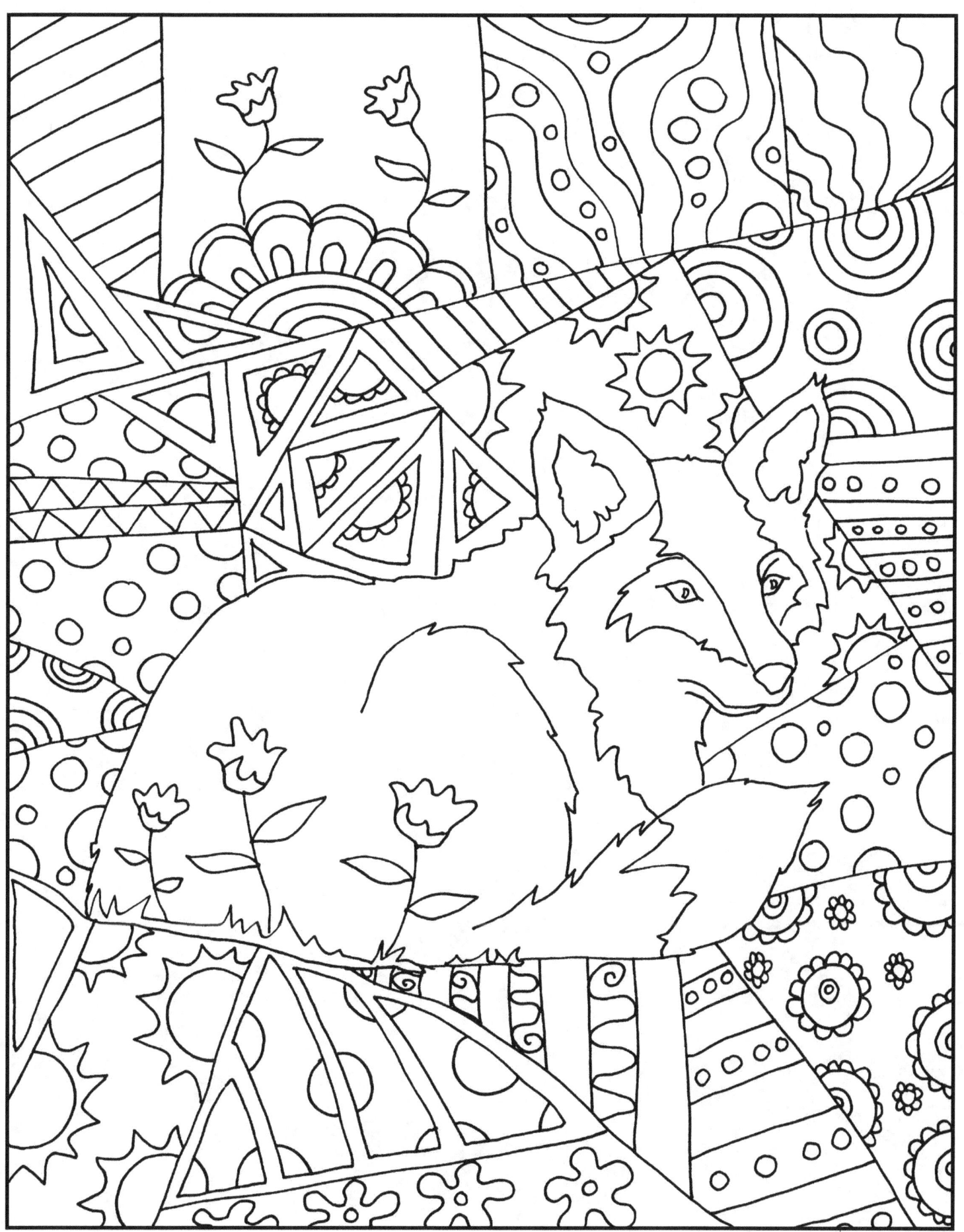

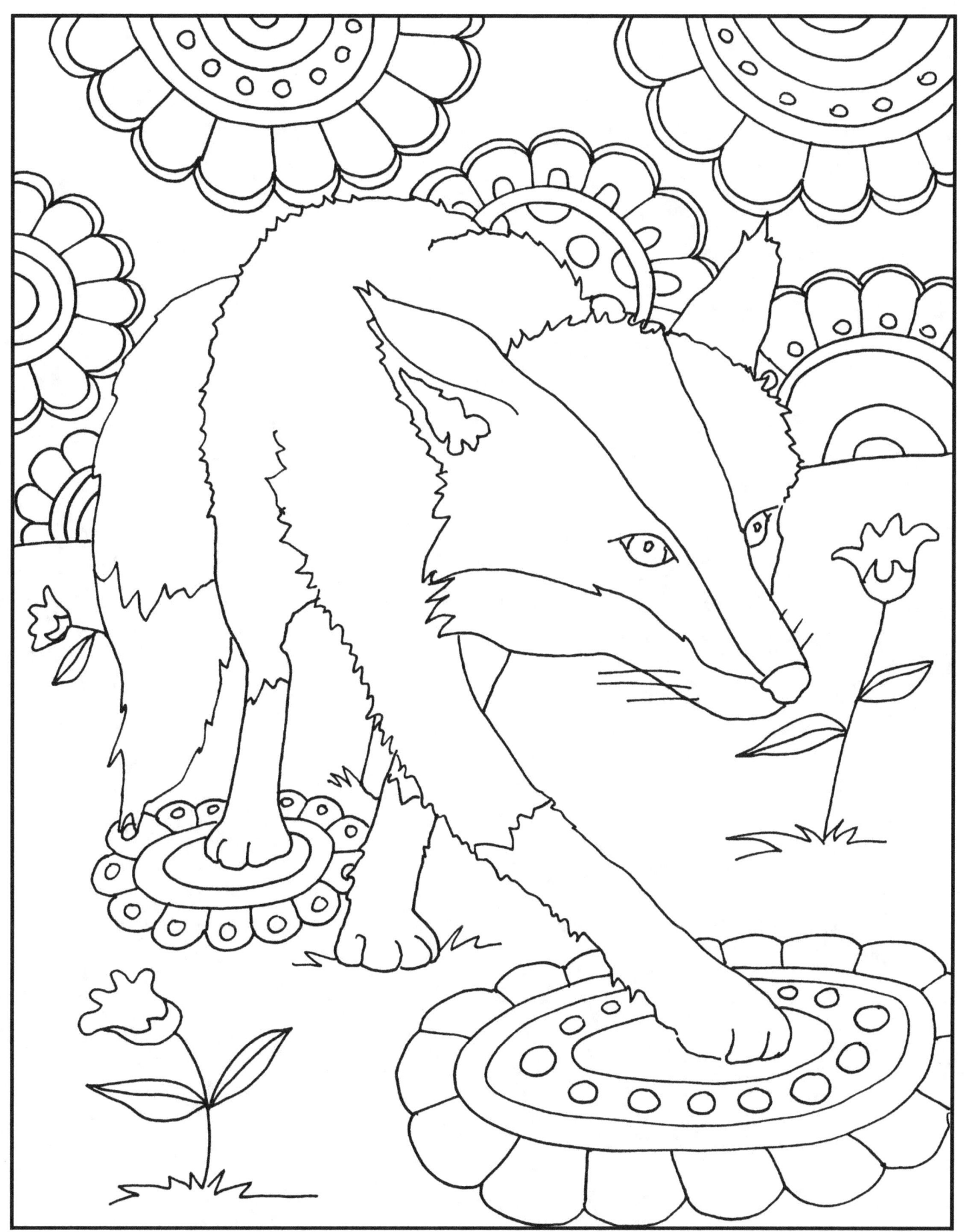

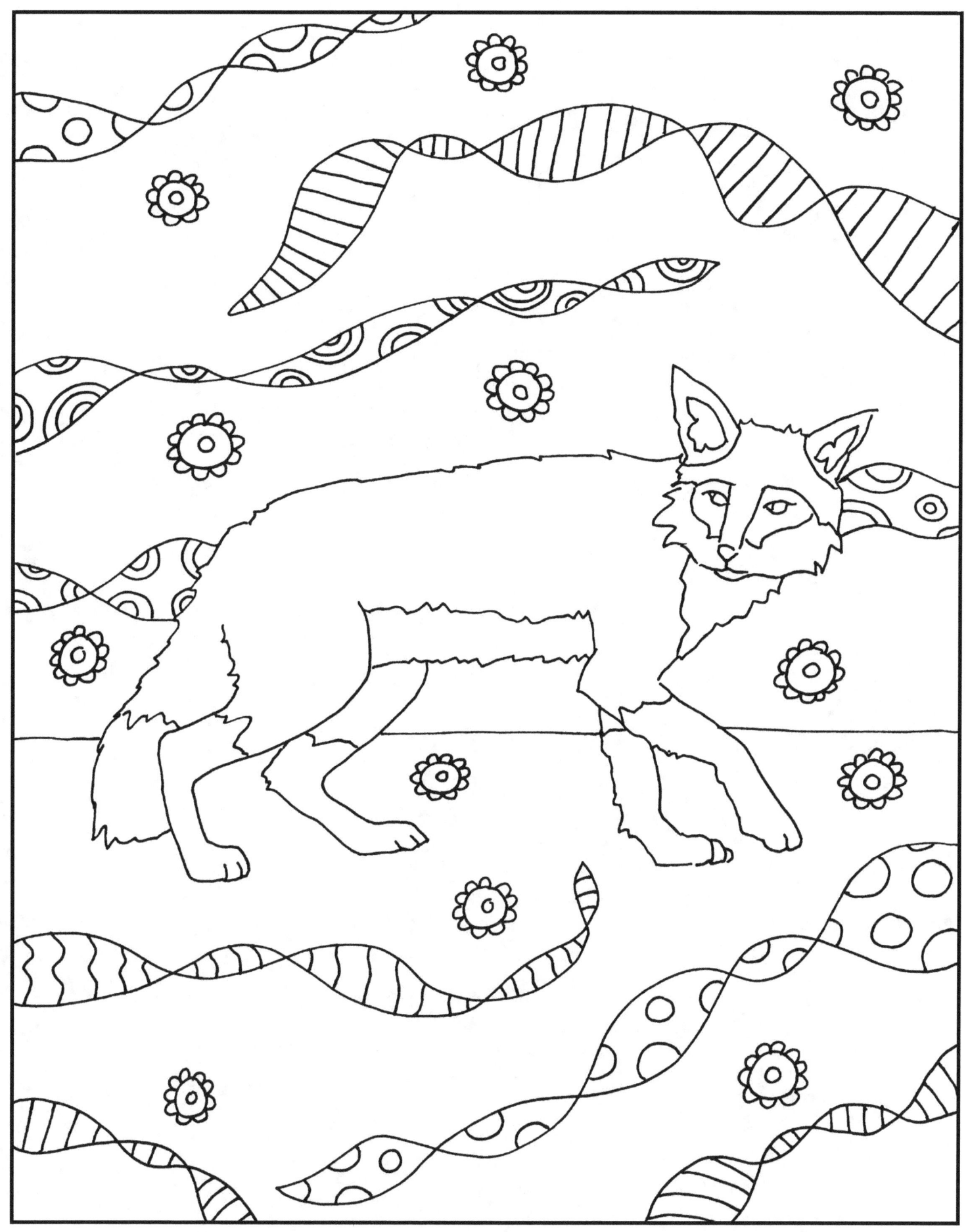

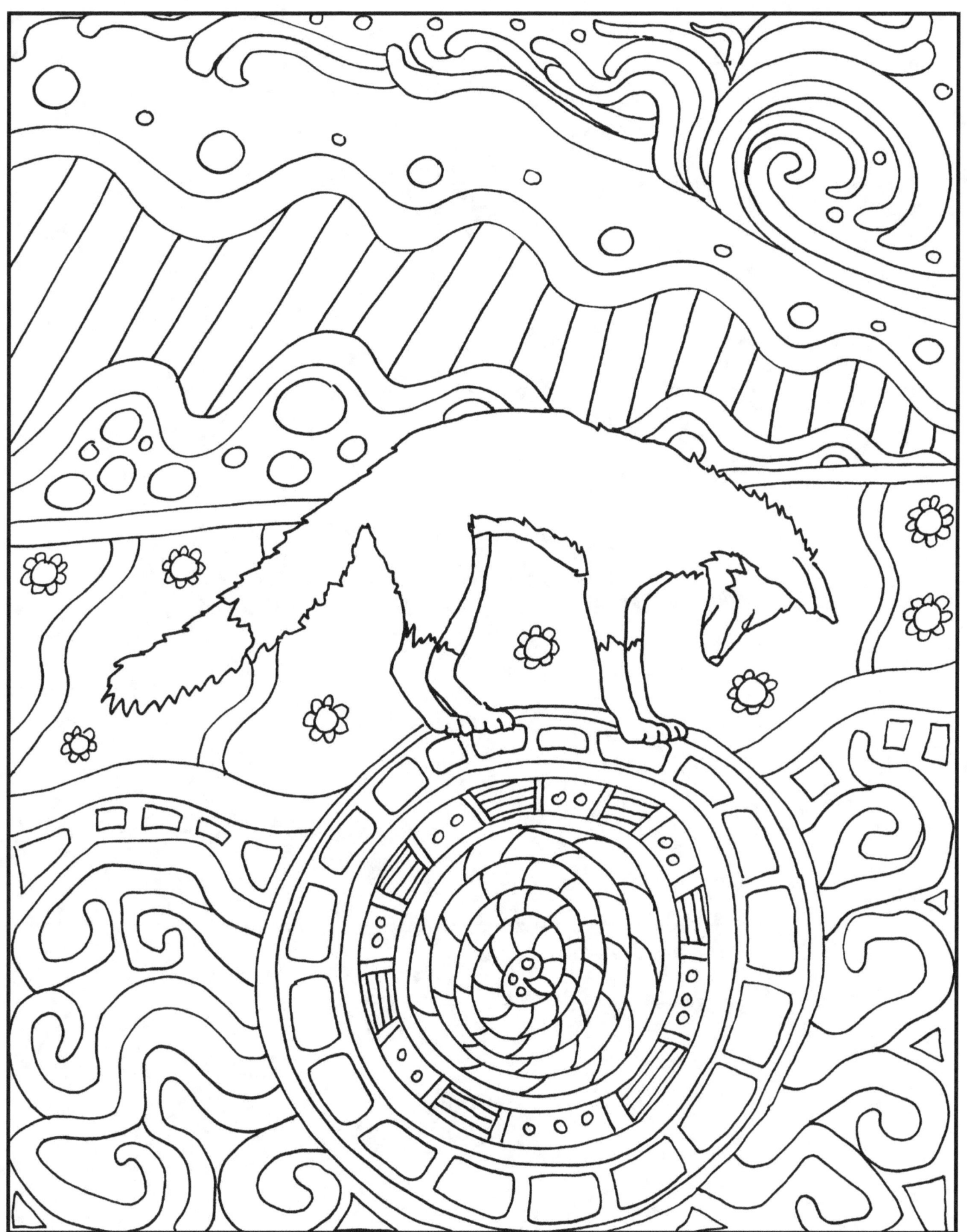

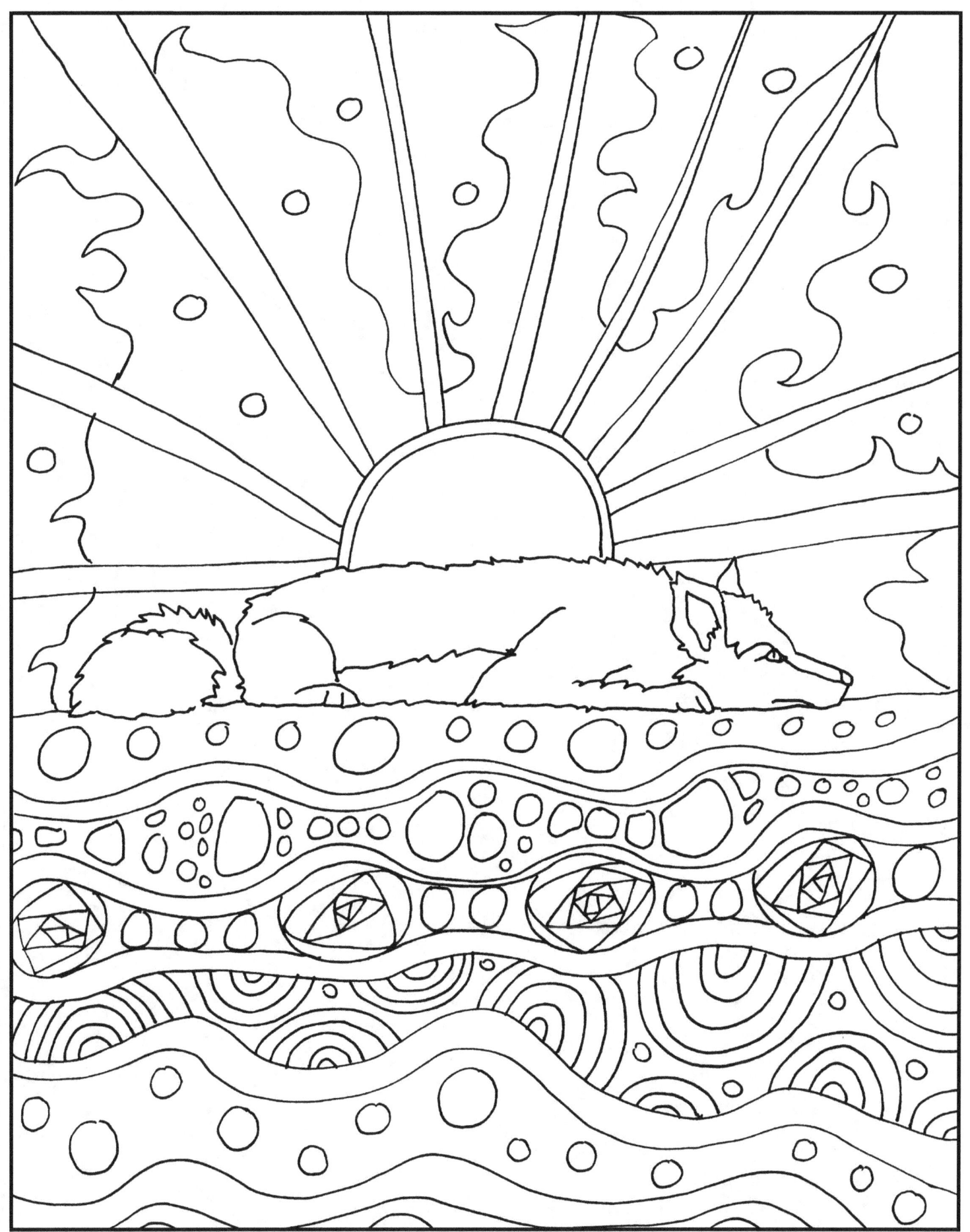

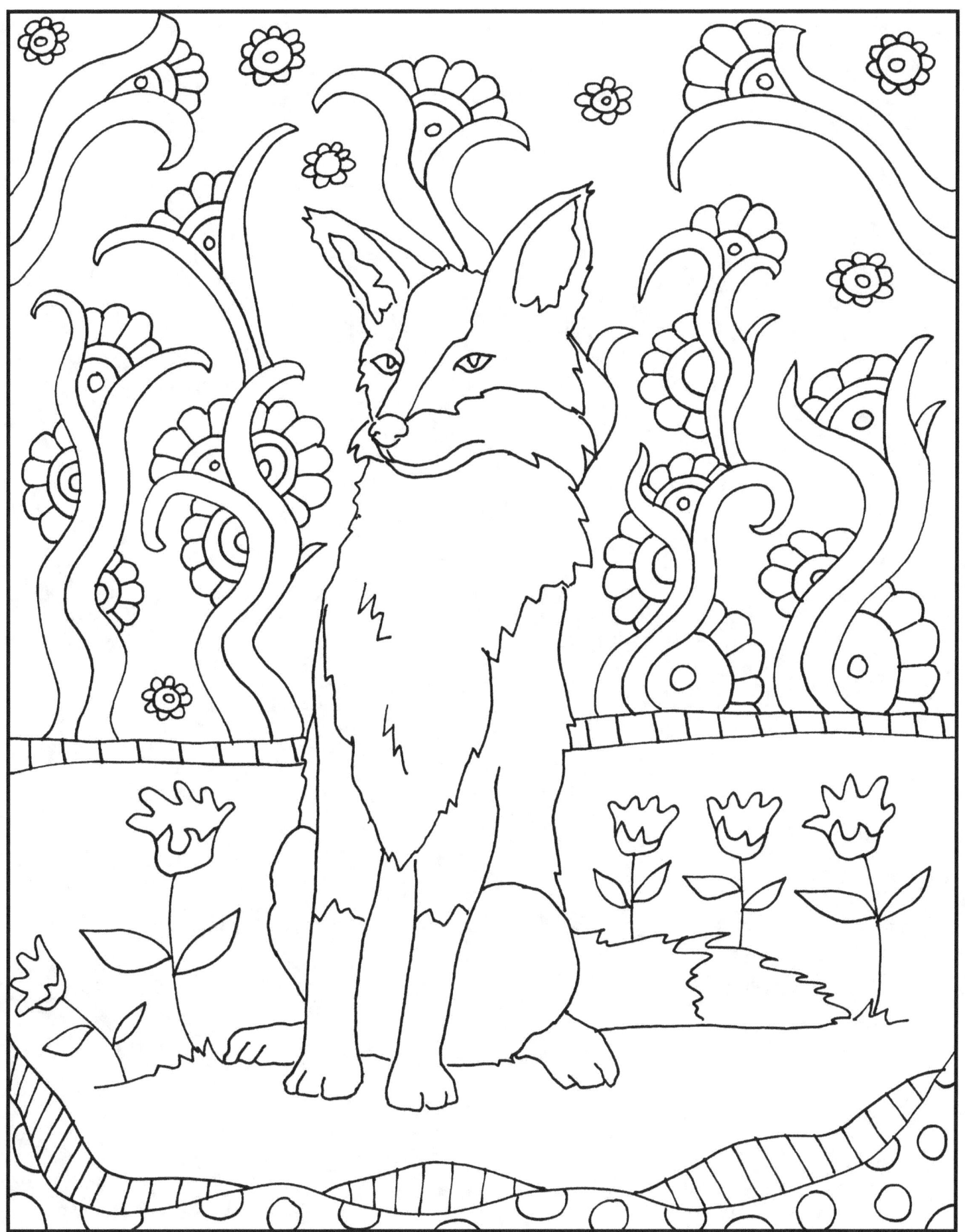

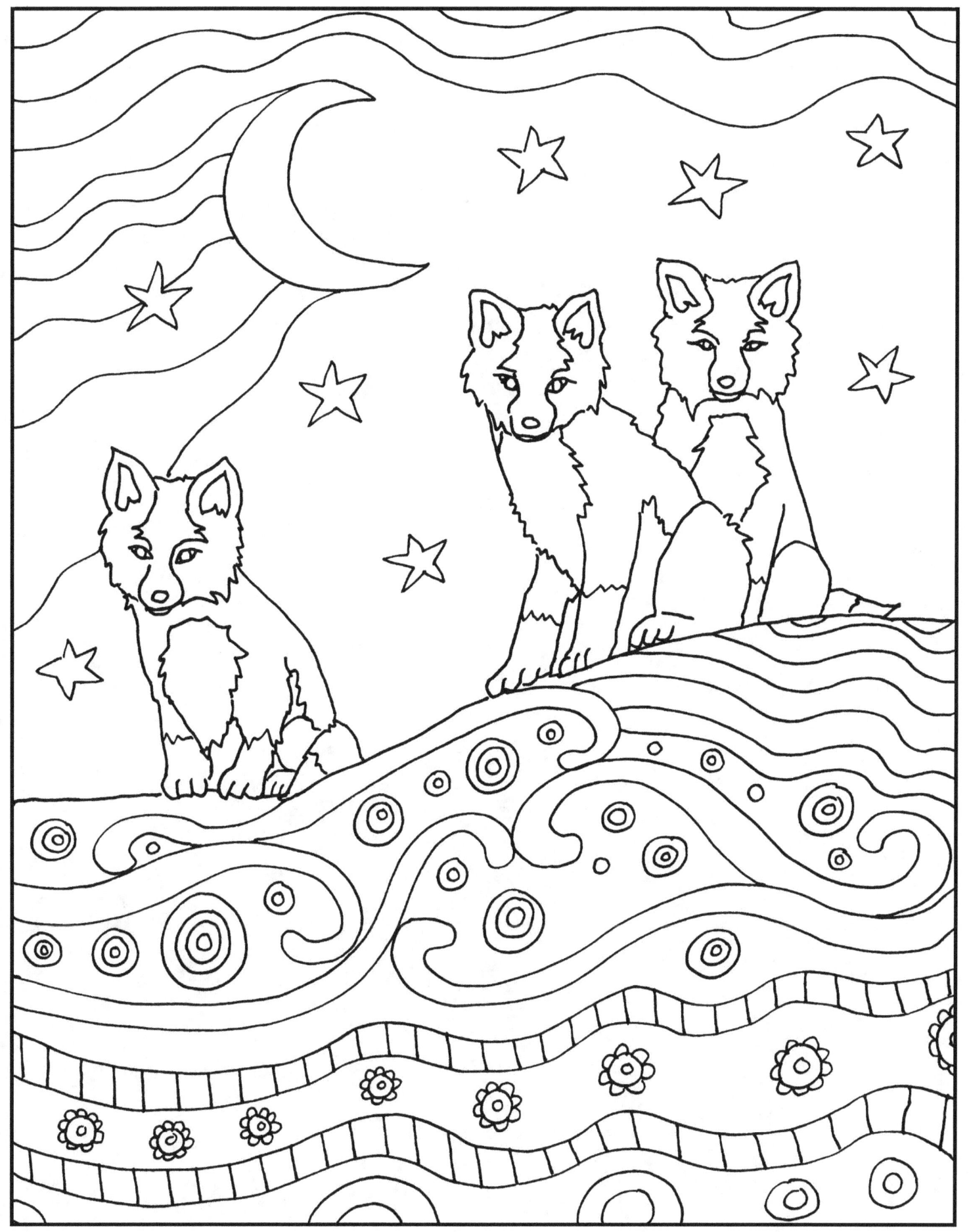

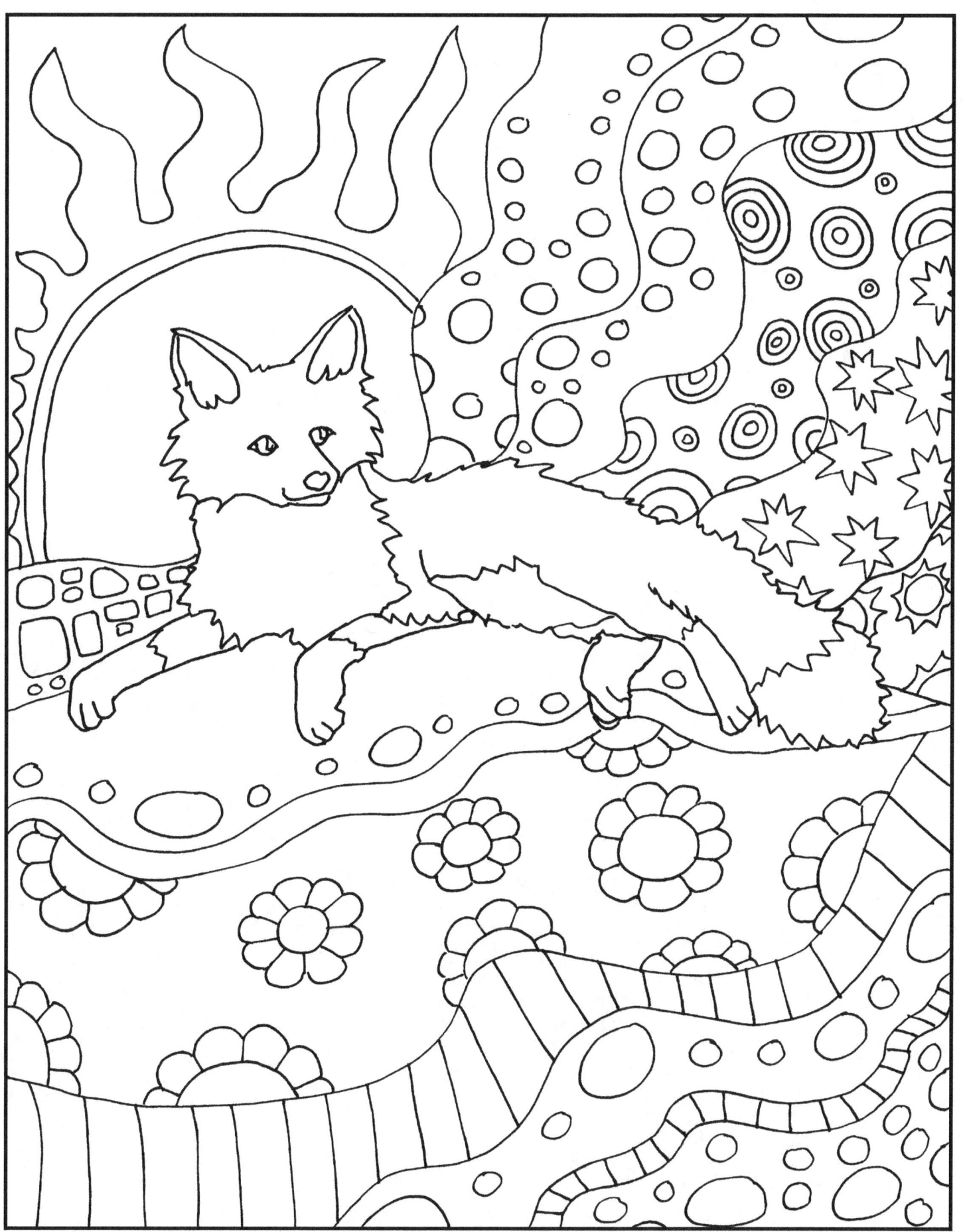

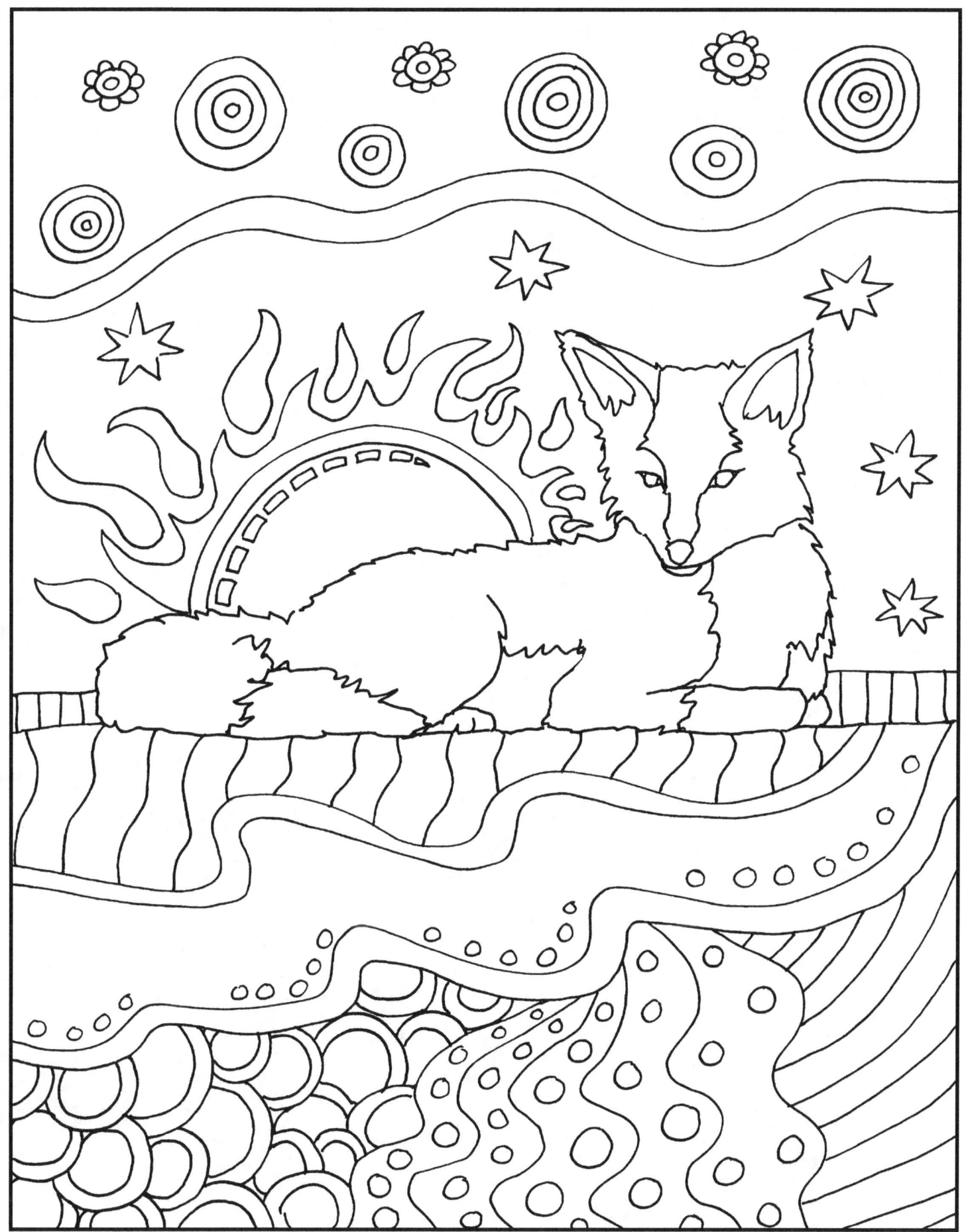

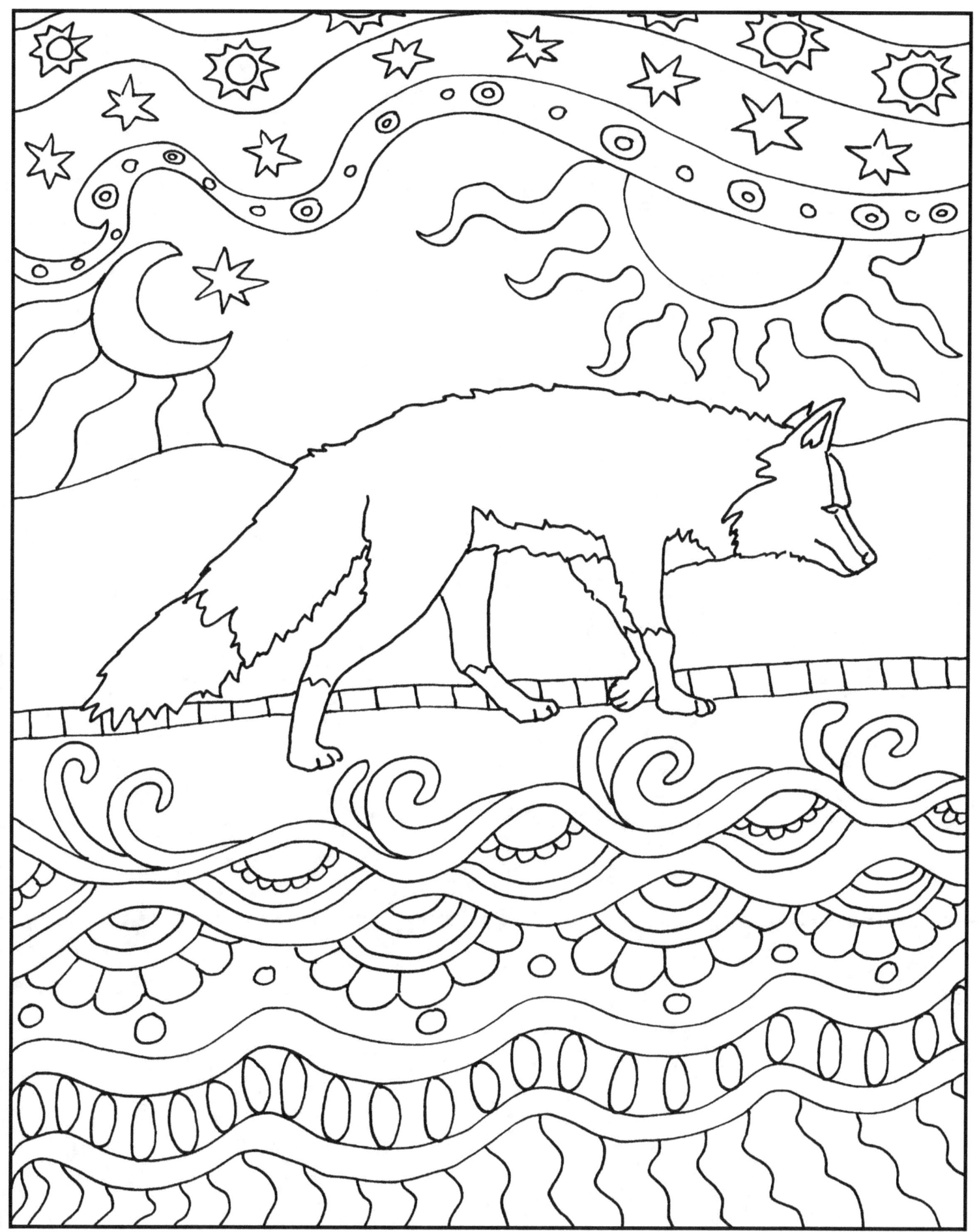

Also Available by Kimberly Garvey

- **Strange Designs** - An adult coloring book for everyone.

- **Strange Little Designs** - A mini/travel adult coloring book.

- **Simple Designs** - An adult coloring book with easier pages.

- **Simple Designs II** - Another adult coloring book with easier pages.

- **Magical Daydreams** - An adult coloring book for everyone.

- **It's Complicated** - A challenging. more detailed book for the daring colorists.

KIMBERLYGARVEY.COM

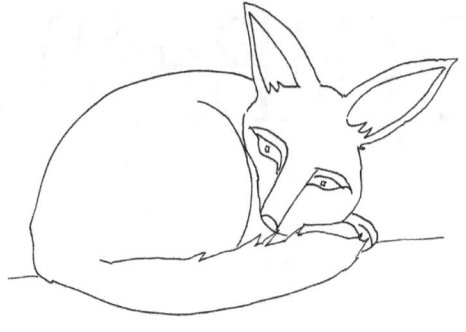

KIMBERLYGARVEY.COM

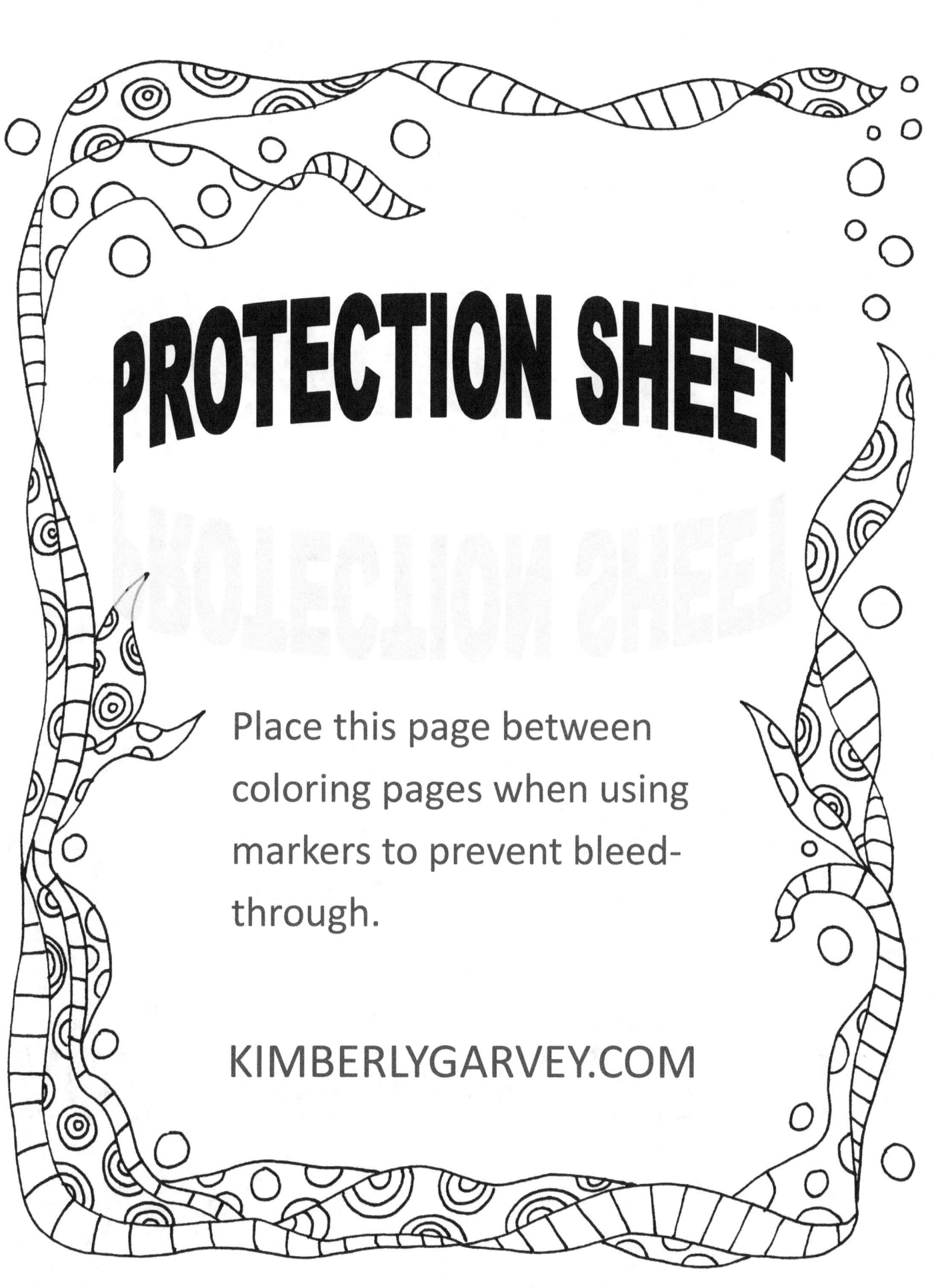

PROTECTION SHEET

Place this page between coloring pages when using markers to prevent bleed-through.

KIMBERLYGARVEY.COM

KIMBERLYGARVEY.COM